MANAGING CLASSROOM PROBLEMS
IN THE PRIMARY SCHOOL

Gerald Haigh has been a teacher since 1961. He was a head in Warwickshire for eleven years. While retaining a base in teaching, he is now a writer and educational consultant, and is well known for his contributions to *The Times Educational Supplement* and *The Independent*.

Managing Classroom Problems in the Primary School

GERALD HAIGH

P·CP
Paul Chapman
Publishing Ltd

Paul Chapman Publishing Ltd
144 Liverpool Road
London
N1 1LA

British Library Cataloguing in Publication Data
Haigh, Gerald
  Managing classroom problems in the primary school.
  1. Great Britain. Primary schools. Classrooms. Discipline
  – For teaching.
  I. Title
  372.110240941

ISBN 1-85396-114-0

Typeset by Burns and Smith Ltd, Derby
Printed by St Edmundsbury Press, Bury St Edmunds
Bound by W.H. Ware & Sons Ltd, Clevedon

ABCDEFG   543210

CONTENTS

PREFACE

In the last resort, you cannot learn teaching from a book, any more than you can learn how to drive by reading a motoring magazine.

Nevertheless, the pressure of teaching practice, or of the early part of a teaching career, is such that many quite obvious truths, techniques and strategies go whizzing by unnoticed. What the educational writer can do to help is to field some of these whizzing principles and set them down so that, away from the classroom, they can be read, studied, accepted or scorned at leisure.

This, simply, is my purpose. There are no definitive answers here, only a set of guidelines and principles which I have tried out over thirty years. Some of them worked for me and may work well for others; a few, perhaps, are to do with my own personality and approach and might not easily transfer to other people and other schools. You never know until you try.

In a way this is a highly personal book, owing little or nothing to any research project or to the practice of others. All the same, if thirty years of teaching taught me anything, it was that there is always something to learn, and with that in mind I freely acknowledge here, and thank, all of those hundreds of colleagues and thousands of, parents and children I have encountered in the seven schools I have worked in and the dozens more I have visited. In particular, I thank the distinguished parade of head teachers for whom, and with whom, I have worked — Dolly Masterson, Ted Grubb, Graham Shaw, Jim Herbert, Bill Rumble, Richard Harris, Bill Evans. There is, in truth, a bit of all of them in me.

Gerald Haigh
Bedworth, 1990

Part I: The Teacher's Task

Being a classroom teacher in the primary school is a stressful, demanding job – let there be no doubt about that. It is within the nature of the task that the teacher has to be on concentrated full alert all the time the children are in the room. There is no opportunity for moments of inattention – for five minutes gazing out of the window or for telephoning a friend in another school. Relaxation comes only at break and lunchtime, and any teacher will swiftly point out the number of times that even these islands of calm are eaten into by the demands of children.

This being so, teachers who wish to survive should come to terms with their own mortality – should realize that the job is difficult and that they are not going to achieve perfection within one year, or even within fifteen. If it helps, they can be told that seasoned headteachers share the same fears, the same black depressions, the same feelings of sheer inadequacy and failure that beset every probationer. Their only advantage is in the fact that experience has taught them to ride out storms, to realize that few problems are terminal and to grasp at various emotional props – the most vital of which is a sense of humour.

Teachers should also take courage and pride in the fact that it is the classroom job – the encounter between pupil and teacher – that is at the heart of education. Everything else in the system, up to and including the papers on the desk of the Secretary of State, are there to make the classroom job possible. It is not so much that the classroom teacher is the most important adult in the system; it is more that without the classroom teacher there is no system. Any visitor, therefore – governor, Member of Parliament, royal – who patronizes the classroom teacher or in any way treats him or her as inferior is committing a breathtaking solecism!

The classroom teacher, therefore, has every reason to feel confident about him or herself. Part of this confidence involves recognizing some basic skills of classroom management. Part also involves knowing that to ask for help is not an admission of weakness or defeat!

1
LOOKING FOR HELP

Feelings of isolation

The life of a primary-school class teacher can sometimes – perhaps surprisingly – be a lonely affair. 'How can this be?' you say, 'When the image of the primary school is that of a small and caring community?' The answer is that it is extremely easy for the most caring of schools to be so busy at its work that assumptions take the place of considered judgements. It can be assumed, for example, that each teacher is content and confident when they are not. This is considerably compounded by the fact that teachers are often inhibited by a professional pride that prevents them from being too forthcoming about their problems. Every teacher aspires to be the one who is liked and respected by every child, and anything that detracts from this tends to get hidden.

This leads (often quite damagingly) to teachers failing to admit when they are having problems. Sometimes they do not admit it even to themselves. When, for example, a teacher has had a bad-tempered encounter with a difficult child during which the child has been rude and disobedient, he or she may well come into the staffroom and 'talk' the encounter out in a way that considerably improves the way he or she handled it. 'No child gets away with that in my classroom! They all know that! You could have heard a pin drop when I'd finished!' The fact is, of course, that, first, the encounter should not have happened at all and, second, that once it did arise it should have been defused before it became a shouting match. That this is a counsel of perfection is not the point. What is the point is not that the teacher should have been perfect but that he or she should have been able to recognize the things he or she did wrong and admit them to him or herself and to his or her colleagues.

The underlying theme here is that teachers are often not as supportive to each other as they think they are. Teachers are, after all, human beings in the workplace, and the competitive nature of the workplace causes people, alas, not only to delight in their own successes but also to get satisfaction from the failures of others. It is as if the presence of someone who performs less well somehow confirms the security of everyone else. A group of salesmen, for example, quite like it when there is one bad performer among them – he takes the flak, he makes them look good and he, not they, is going to get the sack. He is also a good topic for snide gossip: 'Guess what you-know-who did this week!'

Now teachers are not salesmen, and the law of the jungle is not, in a staffroom, quite so near the surface. We have to recognize, however, that the jungle factor is there, to a greater or lesser degree. Teachers who doubt this should do a little self-analysis about, for instance, their inner feelings when watching a colleague having problems with a group of children. Is it all sympathy and a desire to give support? Is there absolutely no smugness hiding away there inside at all?

Another factor that goes against the ability of teachers to give mutual support is the way they work. A primary teacher, typically, goes into a classroom, shuts the door and works all day with thirty children. This is a simplification, but it is deliberately made, because the opposite assumption – that the typical primary teacher works in an open-plan area with a team of colleagues and a large, mixed group of children – is also a simplification. The closed and isolated classroom is even now probably the more typical of the two. It is interesting to see, incidentally, how many teachers have succeeded in converting open-plan classrooms into closed ones by moving the cupboards about. A closed classroom, with a conventional door, is a strong barrier to the development of a supportive network in a school. In an open-plan school, teachers and children can move – sidle, almost – into each other's spaces without seeming to intrude. You cannot, however, open a classroom door and sidle inside without looking extremely obtrusive, not to say silly. The only way to get into a closed classroom is to knock on the door and walk in: a procedure that brings the lesson to a halt and draws the attention of everyone in the room. In a sense, therefore, nobody beyond the class ever sees what really goes on in a closed room, because as soon as someone else goes in the ground rules change – teacher and children all start to behave differently.

This makes it difficult for teachers to be supportive to each other. Consider the practicalities. A teacher in a closed classroom is suffering because of the behaviour of a disruptive pupil. Not only is the pupil himself challenging the teacher, but his behaviour is sparking off other children in the same class, and the teacher–pupil relationship is going downhill at a frightening rate. If the teacher does not actually ask for help – either openly or by coded messages to which colleagues ought to be sensitive – then other colleagues may only have a vague idea of what is going on. They may know that, in general terms, 'Mary is finding those lads difficult', but they may judge that it is a temporary problem arising from inexperience, or they may simply feel that they should not interfere without being asked. What is the outside evidence after all? Noise from the classroom? It has to get pretty bad before people in neighbouring rooms start to worry about it. A generally mutinous attitude from the class is noticeable when, for instance, they are in assembly alongside more relaxed groups? Perhaps, but teachers have a tendency to blame the children themselves for this: 'They were heading that way last year when I had them'. And suppose colleagues do get worried, what do they do? Probably they would approach the head or the deputy, who would then have to decide whether to take action. It will not be an easy decision because it will mean broaching the subject with the teacher on the basis of what might be quite flimsy evidence. If the teacher denies there is a problem, usually by saying something like, 'They're a lively lot but I can cope', then the options are just about closed up.

Teachers who deny their problems do so for a mixture of reasons. Some of them are 'professional' – fear of failing the probationary year, for example, or of not gaining a much-wanted promotion. Others are 'personal' – teaching is an emotional, affective business and feelings of failure bite very hard into the recesses of a teacher's soul. Teachers new to these feelings should take comfort that every single teacher, at every level in the profession, continues to have times of despair and doubt. What is important is that they *must* be shared. Most heads and deputies are sensitive enough to listen. If they are not, there is usually someone on the staff who is. And if all else fails, the local-authority advisers and advisory teachers can be consulted.

Seeking support for individuals

What is also important for this aspect of classroom management is that teachers are able to identify when an individual child starts to present problems severe enough for the teacher to need support. Exactly how this support is sought and provided varies from school to school and authority to authority, but there is usually a way of providing some kind of help up to and beyond the formal procedure of 'statementing' for special needs.

Class teachers have to find the right balance when considering whether or not to start pressing for support. On the one hand if they ask too often, for too many children, their position might start to lack credibility. On the other hand, they have to remember that individual children have suffered in various ways simply because nobody pushed for special provision hard and early enough.

The general principle that any class teacher should be observing is that he or she cannot expect to have a perfect, problem-free group of children. Every teacher either has, or has known, one or two children who take up a great deal of time and energy. In some cases the removal of just one child transforms a class and has a tremendous effect on the teacher's quality of life. It does not follow, however, that the teacher has any right to expect the child to be permanently removed. No teacher has any fundamental right to a perfect class – the age-old professional principle is that you teach whomever turns up.

Nevertheless, it is equally wrong for the teacher to have to battle on alone. In a well-run school there will be a special-needs teacher who should be perfectly aware of which children need extra support. This teacher may well, however, have a demanding timetable, and what knowledge they have is going to come at least in part from the class teachers, either through the school's record-keeping system or through meetings and informal consultations.

Suppose, then, that a teacher is becoming increasingly worried about a particular child – about work, behaviour or both. At what point does the teacher make a request for help? A useful strategy is to make a very early preparatory informal approach direct to the special-needs teacher: 'I'm a bit worried about Jimmy Smith, I might be asking you for some help'. This is a sort of 'testing the water' operation; the teacher cannot be accused of over-reacting to a little difficulty, because he or she is not, in fact, making a request at all. How this is received varies according to the personality of the teacher who is approached, and also according to the workload he or she has. On the one hand, he or she might pick up the request with enthusiasm and act as positively on it as if the request had been a formal one. On the other hand, though, his or her workload may be so great that he or she will automatically, as a simple piece of time management, keep at arm's length any problem that is not placed formally before him or her. 'Well, I shall be here when you want me', is how this latter position is usually defined.

Perhaps the key to deciding when to shout for help lies in the amount of time the 'problem' child is taking up. Every child in a class has an equal right to the teacher's attention, and there comes a point when one child is so enormous a diversion that the other children are starting to suffer. The ones who suffer most, needless to say, are the able and co-operative ones, who can be left to 'get on' and who (too often) end up doing undemanding work because of this.

Pupils may demand attention in various ways. They may, for example, behave in a disruptive way – walking about the room, shouting out, getting into minor fights and disputes. Or they may be perfectly well behaved but be struggling with their work to the extent that they can only do anything at all if the teacher is by their side to prompt and guide.

It is not a bad idea to make a note of the demands such children make – a simple system of ticks against a time-scale will do. This does two things – it reassures the teacher that he or she is not imagining the extent of the problem, and the record provides good supportive evidence when it comes to the time to talk about extra support.

In any case, tick sheet or no, the cry for help, when it is made, has to be backed up with chapter and verse. This is yet another time when vague and woolly judgements – 'He's very disruptive', 'She's miles behind with her reading' – just will not do. The head and the special-needs teacher need all the details – how many times a day is the child disruptive, and in what exact ways? Where is she on the reading scheme, and how is she performing by comparison with others?

What might typically happen, therefore, is this. A class teacher, in her second year in the profession, has a child who has come up from the infants school apparently entirely unable to read. During reading lessons he sits looking around and can only do anything at all with the simplest material when the teacher is sitting with him offering constant encouragement and help. Now there are, of course, various strategies for helping such children. The problem is, though, that the class teacher has another thirty or so pupils to consider, and the provision of what is effectively a separate programme for her non-reader is probably going to take up so much time that the work of her other pupils will suffer. She should not, for example, find herself in the position where she is spending hours in the evening and at weekends preparing or seeking out material for this one child. What she needs is help – in the form of advice, of resources and, if at all possible, of an extra pair of hands in the classroom.

Now what the teacher has to remember at this point is that the resources of any primary school are stretched for most, or all, of the time to the absolute limit. In many schools every teacher is looking after a class and only the head is free of a full-time teaching load. What this means is that from the point of view of the school's management the best way of dealing with any difficult child is for him or her to stay in class and be looked after by the class teacher. A head may, in fact, work to achieve this solution, saying something like, perhaps, 'I know he's difficult, but we've had worse. If he becomes a real problem any time wheel him down the corridor to see me. Do your best till Christmas and we'll look at it again'. If this is said with one hand on the teacher's elbow, propelling them towards the door, it becomes extremely difficult to stand firm. This is why the facts and the arguments have to be marshalled in advance, and it is also why the head has to be pinned down to a proper consultation and not casually accosted in the corridor or at the coffee-machine during break. The teacher has to say, 'When can I see you about Jimmy Smith? I need half an hour to talk to you about him'. If the answer is vague, then the point has to be pushed, if necessary with the support of the deputy head, part of whose job is to oil the wheels of such encounters. 'I've been trying to get half an hour with the head about Jimmy Smith. Can you help me to pin him down? I'm really worried about this child!'

It needs to be said here that classroom teachers need a certain amount of push when it comes to bringing matters to the attention of management. The opposite side of this principle, of course, is that in some schools the teachers with the most push are the ones who get the most support. Good heads have management techniques that help them to avoid this state of affairs, but the fact remains that there are still too many schools where it happens. In this respect schools are no different from any other place of work!

The best way to argue the case is, probably, to concentrate on the damage being done to the rest of the class. The head may be extremely compassionate, and anxious to help Jimmy, but it is still true that nothing will spur him or her into action more than the prospect of complaints from the parents of other children that their sons and daughters are being neglected because of Jimmy Smith. The head will also be concerned about the performance of the whole class on National Curriculum targets.

The teacher with this problem needs, as we have seen, advice, resources and help in the classroom. It is probably best not to ask for all of these, because this is tempting the head to offer advice, which is free, and scrub round the other two, which are not. It is better to plunge straight in and say, 'I cannot operate properly unless there is some classroom help'. The quick answer, often, will be that there is no slack in the system from which any teacher support can be drawn. It is surprising, though, how a really resourceful head can find a bit of time here and there. He or she may, for instance, use some of his or her own time, either to provide support or to release another teacher to provide it. (He or she may already be releasing teachers in rotation for 'marking periods', and if colleagues are sympathetic enough to the problem they may volunteer to use some of this time for support – or at least not object too strongly if the head asks them to do it.) There may be other bits of slack in the system – a part-time teacher may be used in a way that does not look all that productive; the school helper may be available. It does no harm to research such solutions, perhaps, again, talking them over with the deputy head.

Of course, in a well-managed school the whole problem ceases to be a semi-confrontational matter between the individual teacher and the head and is, instead, a whole-school affair, to be discussed openly and ultimately tackled in a collaborative way by a number of colleagues. The fact remains, though, that the attitude of the head is crucial. However collaborative and open the style of management, the head still has one eye on the budget and the resources and, in any case, whoever is making the decision, the teacher making the requests still needs to be arguing from a good base of knowledge and research.

It may be possible to widen the whole discussion: to enlist the help of other teachers who are struggling with similar problems and to argue that either more children be put forward for statementing or that more of the staffing budget be allocated to special-needs support. A self-managing school, under local management of schools, is more than capable of deciding how to allocate its staffing money and has the power to employ more teachers if the will – and the money – is there. At one time when teachers asked their heads for more staff the pet answer was that the school had to work within the staffing pattern set by the authority. This is no longer true – the school's staffing level is set by the governors, in consultation with the head, and if the staff make out a case for more special-needs support then the governors should respond – even if they refuse, they ought to provide some reasons for the answer.

Extra resources are governed by the same principles. If the head and the governors want to spend money on them they have the right to do so. This means that a teacher who is making his or her own pre-reading materials at home may want to ask some questions if, for example, ten brand-new leather footballs suddenly arrive in the games cupboard. All teachers, at whatever level, must become aware of this sort of thing, and must press towards the only sensible answer, which is for resource and staff decisions to be made openly and democratically by everyone who is affected.

At the same time, the danger of opening up a particular problem in this way is that the immediate request will be forgotten. Setting up a general review in response to an immediate need is a well-known political ploy, and can be just a way of buying time in the hope that the difficulty will eventually go away. Always, therefore, the discussion has to be brought back to finding a solution to the problem of Jimmy Smith and his reading. In particular, the very last question the class teacher should ask, whether it be in the head's room or in the democratic staff meeting, is 'What is going to happen next, then?' If necessary, he or she should stay seated when everyone else stands up and gathers their papers together, and keep asking about what is going to be done the next day.

Heads, by the way, are in no position to carp about being treated like this. They usually know that they themselves only get things done by behaving in exactly this way with the authority or with the governors. Class teachers who push a bit are not going to get labelled as troublemakers – rather will they be admired and, ultimately, marked down as allies to be used in battles outside the school!

Action checklist

1. *Share* problems.
2. Identify individual 'problem' children.
3. Gather evidence that will stand up in discussion.
4. Research possible in-school coping strategies.
5. Support a whole-school policy for children with special needs.
6. Do not gossip and moan – be open, be professional, but be persistent!

2
CLASSROOM MANAGEMENT

Management is much talked about these days. Heads go off on management courses, 'senior management teams' have meetings together. The challenges posed by the National Curriculum and by local management of schools are said to place severe 'management' demands on the leadership of a school.

All of this may sit uneasily on a new – or relatively inexperienced – classroom teacher, who feels that his or her problems with the class, although less high-flown than the ones under constant discussion, are nevertheless urgent, worrying and, perhaps, rather more to the educational point.

Schools are becoming considerably more 'collegiate' in structure and democratic in approach – which is to say that heads are, these days, much more ready to listen to their colleagues and to regard them all, whatever their experience, as co-equals in a shared task. If they are to cope (and, indeed, they have very little option) – the very nature of headship now demands that the burden be shared.

What this means is that probationers are now much less likely, should they speak up at a staff meeting, to be put down or openly told to keep quiet (something that has actually happened within my experience). Today's 'young' teacher – by which I mean young in experience, not necessarily young in years – is importantly *empowered* in a way that his or her predecessors never were.

How do you use this power? What should be the priorities of young teachers as they join in the discussion at staff meetings, and take part in school-based INSET sessions?

There is, it seems to me, one over-riding priority the whole school ought to keep in mind, and that the young classroom teacher is almost uniquely qualified to speak on, and that is the need to bear in mind constantly the learning experience of the individual child. Staff meetings, management planning, school development can all, if care is not taken, operate in an educational stratosphere where all the talk is of budgets, statements of aims, staff structures and the need to market the school. What matters in a school, though, is the point at which teacher and pupil come together, and the classroom teachers in a school are, so to speak, put there to ensure that this meeting point is always the focus of discussion.

Consider, for a moment, the job of a classroom teacher. He or she works within onerous but easily defined limitations. These are as follows:

- *Time* Work has to be done within set time limits, on an hourly, daily, termly and yearly basis.
- *Resources* The books, paper, paint and all the other materials allocated to the teacher have to be used efficiently so that the maximum benefit is gained.
- *People* The class itself is 'given'. Teachers may wish they had 20 friendly intellectuals instead of 32 awkward and noisy rebels, but the choice is not theirs. They may also be able, to some extent, to manage the time of some adults – parent volunteers or the school helper.
- *Space* Teachers have to manage their classrooms and any adjoining open areas in the best way to achieve what they want.

All of these things have to be managed in such a way that the learning experience of each of the 32 children is the best possible within the set limits. At all times, the teacher's vision has to be dominated by a mental picture of the individual child working through the school day. If he or she is successful the children will learn well, in a stress-free environment. There will be no shouting, no moments of chaos, no moments when the teacher does not know what to do next. Disruptive behaviour will be at a minimum because at any given moment each child will always be challenged by a task that is at the same time enjoyable, stimulating and achievable.

This, needless to say, is an ideal – the very description that is going to raise some ironic cheers from readers. It is, nevertheless, an ideal that has to be kept firmly in mind as something to aim for. The teacher – or head, or Secretary of State – who is not working towards an ideal mental model is, almost by definition, adrift and potentially failing.

What is particularly relevant to the theme of this book, of course, is that if the teacher's management schemes and structures start to collapse, then the kind of atmosphere is created in which problems and disruptions thrive, and which leads to crises and parental dissatisfactions.

It is useful to take the management tasks one by one.

Time

Time management is a problem for all teachers and heads. The fundamental problem in teaching is the constant presence of lots of lively children with a stream of pressing demands. The result is that it is too easy to lapse into a 'reactive' method of working where the teacher or head gets through simply by responding to a day-long series of problems and crises. Every teacher knows what it is like to finish the day having failed to accomplish almost any of the targets set at the beginning.

Example A teacher decides to start the day by going in and doing ten minutes of mental arithmetic – right at the start, before registration or anything. She goes into the classroom mentally rehearsing the first question, only to be met, as the children come in, by a bitterly weeping boy accompanied and supported by six of his friends all of whom are talking at once. She has to decide within seconds whether the boy is hurt or simply upset, and make a quick coping plan to deal with him. While she is doing this, the rest of the class come in and immediately, because she is distracted, embark on a variety of other activities – reading, talking, showing each other treasures or adding to the band of 'witnesses' at her desk. Within two seconds the witnesses are all indignantly shouting each other down. While this is going on a child appears at her elbow with a note from the head to which a brief, but immediate reply is needed. At her other elbow appears another child from the class next door wanting to borrow the paper slicer. A number of children overhear this request and there is a chorus of volunteers, each of whom knows, for absolute certain, that the paper slicer is in a different place.

How the teacher sorts all this out – and she will, if she keeps calm and maintains a mental list of priorities – is almost irrelevant. The point is, though, that her ten minutes of mental arithmetic, which was going to be the start of an absolutely rigid, sacrosanct daily routine, have by now gone, for it is time to do the register and get to assembly!

It is not difficult to spot the kind of classroom problems that will arise out of the amiably chaotic scene I have just described. In any class there are children who will, if unsure of what to do, get up to something irritating, like pinching each other or creeping about under the desks. In themselves these activities are not particularly threatening; what happens, though, is that they can lead, in seconds, to lost tempers and the spectacle of angry children wrestling on the classroom floor, too far gone in temper to listen to reason.

There is no simple answer to this – it is a matter of thinking the problem right through and considering not just 'how to do ten minutes of mental arithmetic' but 'how to do ten minutes of mental arithmetic in the real world of the classroom'. The answer probably is that first thing in the morning is the wrong time to do it. What children need at that time is a routine that will encourage them to come in and settle down without the need for much teacher intervention. They need to feel that there is a clear task to be done, and that the materials for doing it are at hand. 'Read your book' is probably not enough. It will suffice for some children, but there are others who will, if expected to read, use an open book as a kind of talisman to keep the teacher away while indulging in lots of other activities, such as surreptitious name-calling across the room that may flare up later in the day into something more serious. No, what children need first thing in the morning is a clear, achievable task, preferably to be done in co-operation with one or two more. Doing the daily weather recording is one obvious job; another is checking the availability of materials to be used later in the day. And, of course, if children have been helped towards independence in their learning, there will be work assignments to be done that can be embarked on or continued with the minimum of fuss and referral to the teacher. What is needed is the establishment of a routine that assumes that children will come in and get settled down to clearly defined tasks.

It is not that the ten minutes of mental arithmetic cannot be done – it can, and arguably it should. The point is that it needs to be inserted into the day's routine at a time when there are going to be no interruptions – which means, effectively, in the middle of a session.

Resources

Again this is largely a matter of planning. Get it right and the class runs smoothly. Get it wrong and there are hiccups, delays and frustrations – all of them potentially leading to disruption. One of the best tests of a teacher's ability to manage resources is seen in his or her preparation for a class art lesson. This may involve rearranging the furniture, doling out powder paint into small amounts for each group of children, preparing brushes and paper, covering desks with newspaper, getting aprons ready for the children and various other small but highly important operations. Well-organized teachers start by giving themselves enough time to do the job – either by arriving early or by working into break or lunchtime. They also enrol a band of helpers from their classes – the same ones every time, tried and trusted and ruthlessly efficient. In addition, they always have enough materials in their stock areas, having kept a careful eye on things – again with the help of pupils – and called up replacement items well in advance.

Ill-organized teachers arrive in their classrooms at the same time as the children and then attempt to get the room ready amid a gradually deteriorating atmosphere of chaos and confusion. Their insistence on taking every second of their lunchhours or on not arriving in school at 8.15 a.m. may be understandable, but the problems that result more than wipe out any of the pleasure to be had from a few moments of extra relaxation!

It is possible, by dint of good organization, to get the best of both worlds – to have the full lunch hour and also be well prepared. The way to achieve this is to organize the classroom resources in such a way that the children become accustomed to fetching them and using them in an independent and responsible way. Thus the teacher would prepare a sheet saying 'Art. You will need the following . . .' The children then busy themselves, as groups, getting their own materials ready. The step beyond this does not specify what materials the children will need, but encourages them to make their own decisions about resources based on the nature of the task they have to do. Helping children towards this kind of independence requires that the teacher be very well organized but, in return, when it is all running smoothly, the teacher will be able to get through the day without having to do any major resourcing exercises, devoting his or her time instead to helping the children learn.

People

Managing people really means leading them in such a way that they give of their best and also that they help each other to achieve. There seems little doubt that the key to successful classroom work these days lies in collaborative working in groups. Thus teachers have to manage their group work in such a way that slower pupils are helped, able ones stretched and the spirit of collaboration is continually reinforced. And the key to all *this* lies in the nature of the group-work tasks that are set.

The message is, then, that time spent on classroom organization – thinking about the way time is filled, the availability of resources and the use of challenging group tasks – is repaid in lessening of conflict and disruption. What this means, effectively, is that the time-honoured notion of 'class control' is not the whole story. The ability to dominate 35 children by force of personality, while often admired, is not given to everyone. As a skill, though, it has its limitations: carried to absurdity it may lead to a class of children sitting doing nothing for long periods of time while their teacher simply exerts the power of control. There is no doubt, incidentally, that exactly this used to happen quite frequently, and probably still does. Even more common is the kind of lesson where children do unchallenging and time-filling work while being 'held down' by their teacher's ability to 'control'. Sadly, but understandably, silent and highly controlled lessons of this kind are likely to be admired by outsiders as well as by people within the profession who ought to know better.

The ability to keep the children working busily all day is, though, even more important though less well recognized. The hopeful message here is that it is a skill – or a set of skills – that can be learnt and practised. The good classroom teacher may or may not be a charismatic person who can silence a room by blinking. He or she will most certainly, though, be a good organizer. Teachers in trouble should always cling to the undoubted truth that they cannot shout their way out of it, but they can certainly organize their way out of it.

Space

There are decisions to be made, for example, about the arrangement of pupils' tables or desks. Conventionally, in the junior school, tables are pushed together so that children sit round them in groups. Quite often, though, the teacher's style of working simply does not suit this arrangement – she may want to stand at the blackboard for substantial periods of time, or base herself at her desk. With a 'grouped' layout, this may mean that children are getting stiff necks from craning round to see her. Ideally, classroom furniture would be light enough to be easily moved around. In practice, the best that the teacher can achieve is some sort of compromise which preserves the group layout, but which also makes it possible for the room to have a 'focus' at which she can stand and be seen. At the same time, there must be access to all parts of the room. All of this may take a good deal of trial and error, and through it the children should be consulted and not taken for granted as though they themselves are part of the furniture.

One essential for the junior classroom is some sort of quiet, carpeted corner where children can sprawl and sit and read. If the room does not have

one already, it is not too difficult to arrange w
cushions borrowed and cadged. Again, the ch.
this, and they will take up the project with grea
   The important thing is to take nothing for gran.
rooms have a teacher's desk in the same place
everlasting precedent has been set. The teacher's des.
perhaps be discarded altogether. Neither do move
storage units have to stay where they were put five year.
the furniture in a classroom is a challenge, which respor.
and a bit of sideways thinking.

Action checklist

---

1. All management in education starts at the level of the individual child.
2. The class teacher is directly and continuously in touch with children as learners, and therefore has a vulnerable and onerous management task.
3. Manage time; manage resources; manage people; manage space. Do all this effectively and the classroom will work.
4. Don't shout your way out of trouble; *organize* your way out of it!
5. Use time effectively. In particular, do not create sterile marking tasks. The teacher who is a 'marking martyr' is simply badly organized. Look for self-checking and self-assessment strategies – and remember that an hour spent marking is an hour less for preparation. Which is the more effective?

Part II: Children's Problems

3
BULLYING

On the subject of bullying, it is possible to make a generalization that goes something like this. Are you worried about bullying? If not, then you should be, because there is *always* bullying. If you think there is not, or if you do not think about it at all, then your tranquility is being bought at the expense of the unhappiness of a significant number of your pupils.

Perhaps this is an over-simplification. Perhaps there really are schools in which the children, without any intervention by adults, get on well with one another, protecting the weak and cherishing their individuality. Frankly, though, I doubt it. Similarly, it is possible to believe that there are schools where all the children come to school all the time, staying away only when they are really ill. Again, frankly, I doubt it. At 9.10 a.m., in a local post office, a woman turned from the counter and met a friend in the queue. After the initial greeting, her first words were, 'I had trouble with him this morning. Didn't want to go to school again!'

Her friend expressed sympathy, and asked what the matter was.

'Another lad keeps getting on at him. Mark Thomas.'

'Oh, I've heard the name,' said the friend. 'You'll have to see the teacher.'

'I've been down twice.' (This only two weeks into term.) 'She's had a word with Mark Thomas, but it doesn't stop.'

There are all kinds of significant things in this conversation, held, so far as the women were concerned, outside the hearing of a teacher. One is the degree of concern the problem was causing. The mother of the reluctant lad looked worried – her son's distress was right there in the forefront of her mind. Then there was the fact not only that she knew the name of the bully, but also that the other mother recognized it too – not an uncommon state of affairs. The most disturbing thing, though, was that although she had gone to school to sort the problem out (going by the book, as it were) the bullying was continuing unabated. Nothing could illustrate more clearly that the most fundamental characteristic of bullying is its sheer tenacity as a phenomenon, and the amount of time, effort and determination required to root it out.

The archetypal bully was probably Flashman in *Tom Brown's Schooldays* – remember all that blanket tossing and scorching in front of the fire? Such things – and much, much worse – undoubtedly went on in the public schools then and in the years that followed. What is interesting, though, is that the author's attitude to Tom's plight is still common today. What Hughes, effectively, says is that while Flashman's conduct is evil, and deserving of the punishment that inexorably arrives, Tom's ordeal at his hands is not only inevitable but a stern test of his nerve and character.

Many parents take the view that bullying is a natural part of school life, and deal with it not by coming to school to talk but by encouraging their children to 'stand up to' whoever is bullying them. Looked at objectively it is a strategy with some attractions. It avoids, for example, putting the child victim into the visible position of having to be looked after in school by his or her parents. And it does, if it works, encourage self-reliance. The common assumption that bullies are cowards and that one set-piece occasion when victim turns on bully will be enough to end the victim's ordeal has enough truth in it to keep it viable.

Indeed, some schools in the past would encourage this 'standing-up' solution by setting up organized fights in the boxing ring, adding to the accepted wisdom that the right way to deal with bullying was to brace up the victims so that they ceased to be attractive targets.

There are, needless to say, all kinds of problems with this approach. Not least is the fact that many victims really are, come what may, not able to 'stand up to' their tormentors. This is because the dominance of bully over victim is far from being just physical. Many bullies are physically smaller and weaker than their victims, and in any case there are levels of bullying that have no physical component at all. The key to the bully's success lies in his or her moral and emotional domination of one or more victims. And while any particular bully may have more victims than surrounding adults suspect, they are still a minority. What distinguishes the children who are not victims from those who are is not their physical prowess but that they are quite simply unaffected by and detached from the bully's influence.

The implication of this is that any school will contain not just identifiable bullies but also identifiable bullying victims. There are complications of course, such as that some bullies are at the same time the victims of other bullies.

The end result, though, is a great deal of unhappiness. Make no mistake, being the victim of a bully or a group of bullies can be the most traumatic experience of a person's whole life, making a mockery of the notion of childhood as a carefree and happy time. A bullied child wakes up thinking about it, is often miserable at breakfast, fearful on the way to school and on the way home and terrified on the playground. He or she has sleepless nights and, perhaps, various feigned or psychosomatic aches and pains. Work suffers, participation in school events suffers, and scars are left that may still be visible well into adult life, affecting relationships and working life in all manner of ways.

This horrifying picture needs to be painted because teachers need to be convinced, first, of the existence of bullying, then of its seriousness and, finally, on the need to do something about it. 'There is no bullying here,' a head proudly says to a parent or visitor. Heads who say this are either naïve or are deliberately averting their gaze. They were certainly never bullied themselves at school. I think it highly unlikely that there exists any school with no bullying any more than that there is a factory or large office or college that does not have one or two characters who operate by making life unpleasant for anyone who succumbs to their influence.

This is not the same as saying that bullying is inevitable and that schools have to put up with it. On the contrary, the whole-school team, teaching and non-teaching staff, must have the aim of eliminating bullying.

How do you recognize it?

Bullying, by its very nature, is a secret affair. Children are not pushed up against the wall and pinched and punched in front of their teachers. If they are, it is likely that what is going on is another kind of violence altogether – equally unwanted, but probably easier to deal with. Many schools rarely, if ever, see bad-tempered, openly carried out acts of violence like this, which is why, I suspect, they claim to have 'no bullying'. In fact, physical attacks by bully against victim are often rare and are always carried out away from the gaze of authority. The main ingredient of bullying is intimidation based on the fear of such attacks. As the result of just one attack a child may be afraid to go home from school every single day, simply because the bully's technique is to keep alive, by threats and hints, the possibility of its happening again. The victim, too, may reduce the frequency of attack by living defensively – staying near to teachers and dinner supervisors, going home with an adult. The fear, however, will remain so long as the possibility of attack remains, and so long as the bully can continue to exert other kinds of influence.

This is not to play down the possibility of real violence. Some bullying does indeed consist of beatings in the toilet, or of various kinds of youthful torture – lockings in, tyings up, soakings, muddyings. It still remains true, however, that the real damage to the victim arises out of the sheer permanence and oppressiveness of the fear of something happening.

The most important prerequisite for dealing with bullying is disclosure. Children have to be emboldened to speak up. The pressures against speaking up are great. 'Telling tales' or 'grassing' goes against not only childhood conventions, but is also part of the whole dubious structure of adult ethics.

Crucial to the disclosure of bullying is the building of a school ethos that encourages it. School has to be a warm and caring place where, above all, teachers listen to children and have time for them. As part of this structure, the individual teacher must make time for listening to children and must learn to read the signals that say a child is wanting to talk about something.

Very importantly, bullying should be made an open subject in school and in class. The teacher should speak, as frequently as seems necessary, about bullying, saying over and over again that he or she and the head and everyone else want to help but that it is necessary to speak up. Anyone who has doubts about the extent to which bullying is a problem would do well to see the intense interest children take when the teacher speaks about it. The hush that falls, and the serious expressions on the faces of the young listeners, tell an unmistakable tale.

To help overcome the reluctance to speak, children should be given several 'channels' of disclosure. They can talk to their class teacher, to the head, to the deputy head, to a teacher on playground duty, to a dinner lady, to the caretaker, provided that each person in this group is aware of the importance of what they are hearing, and passes it on. Children can also be urged to speak to their parents – 'If you can't tell anyone in school, tell your mum or dad and they will tell me'. This assumes that parents know the school's attitude, and are sufficiently confident to come to school with the problem – which, in turn, presupposes that the school's views on violence and bullying are made clear at every opportunity.

In class

Among the class teacher's major aims ought to be two that, if achieved to any significant degree, will not only help to prevent bullying but will immeasurably improve every aspect of his or her work. The first of these is to enable each child in the class to feel that he or she has a special relationship with the teacher. The second is to help the class towards the feeling that they are a 'family', where mutual support and a network of understanding can be found.

To a great extent, of course, these two aims are interdependent, and neither of them is at all easy to achieve. Neither, though, are they necessarily magical states attainable only by 'gifted' teachers with ill-defined attributes of personality. There are class-management techniques that will help.

Knowing each individual child, for example, can be approached by building in some time to talk to each one. 'Private talk with the teacher', if introduced into the routine, will become a valued part of class life. It can be done at break, at lunchtime, after school or at any similar convenient moment. There are many demands on a teacher's time, and this seems to be adding to them. However, this is one activity that is entirely worth while; the investment of time will be repaid in reduction of classroom stress and confrontation. A new teacher, especially, should make time during the first two or three weeks to have ten or fifteen minutes with each child in the class, talking about hobbies, family, sport, music or whatever. The aim is to make each child feel that he or she shares some particular thing with teacher in a special way – 'Teacher has a cat, I have a cat; teacher is called Elizabeth, I am called Elizabeth; teacher likes The Who; I like The Who'.

Getting to this position with the whole class is by no means an unattainable objective. It can all be as systematic as the teacher likes – the 'special relationship' facts can be put on a card index, or on notes in the mark book, or even on a computer file if that seems easiest. Then from time to time the teacher can look at the list to check that he or she is keeping the various links alive in conversation – joking in front of the whole class, perhaps, or having a quiet word on the way down to lunch. Good teachers have always been good at this, but they have often done it almost instinctively. By applying a bit of classroom management, however, the technique becomes much more widely available.

The second aim – that of building a 'family' feeling in class – comes largely from spending time with the class as a whole. So much primary work is done individually and in groups that it can become difficult for a class to perceive itself as a unit. The teacher should, therefore, find times during the day when the whole class – perhaps sitting out of their places, on a carpet – can be together to talk to the teacher and discuss the events of the day. Problems such as bullying and fighting will often come up in such sessions – the more exposure they have the better.

Getting the school and the class ethos right are at the root of preventing bullying – the net result, if it all works, is not only that the aggression within the potential bully is defused but also that the rest of the class are more mutually supportive and protective. It cannot end there, though. There have to be practical, management measures to address the problem.

Supervision

Bullies thrive in unsupervised, unstructured activities and in unnoticed spaces. It follows that the school should reduce these to the absolute minimum. Consider, for example, the routine for starting the day. Typically, the children arrive from about 8.30 a.m. onwards – in some schools the playground is already well populated at that time, usually by children who want a game of football before everyone else arrives. At about 8.50 a.m. a teacher goes out and blows a whistle. The children stand still, or line up, and then walk into the building, visiting the toilet and hanging up their coats before walking along to class. Very few schools would admit to any major disorderliness in their procedure, and yet there are all kinds of opportunities in it for the bully to operate. The time before school starts, for example, may be in effect a totally unsupervised version of playtime. And where children line up by classes, and a teacher is supervising perhaps six or eight lines, there is often surreptitious pushing and pinching. Some schools find it more practical not to line the children up at all but to have them stand where they are when the whistle blows, and then go in from there. Other schools reject whistle-blowing and bell-ringing and simply allow the children to walk into school as they arrive – though this system presents supervision problems of its own. Once off the playground, though, whatever system is used, the other potential danger points are the toilets and cloakrooms – traditional bully territory. A little further on there may be time spent waiting outside or inside the classroom for the teacher to arrive.

Clearly what all this needs is tighter supervison. There is much to be said, for example, for having a duty teacher on the playground from 8.45 a.m. or even earlier. Similarly, there may be a need for more playground supervision at break and lunchtime, and for teachers to be around the cloakrooms, corridors, entrance halls and toilets during breaks and at the beginning and end of sessions. In some schools children are not just sent in from the playground but are met and escorted in by their teachers. All of this reduces to a minimum the amount of time that children are unsupervised.

The problem about all this, of course, is that it puts an extra burden on the teacher, who is already under pressure from a thousand directions. For the class teacher, busy all day with thirty or so lively children, breaktimes and lunch are precious moments of peace, anticipated and sorely needed. Increasing the amount of playground supervision in a small school will inevitably make serious inroads on this time. This loss of time, though, has to be balanced against the time and energy spent on sorting out problems caused by insufficient supervision. In many schools, for example, teachers have returned to some form of lunchtime supervision simply out of frustration with the amount of time spent each afternoon on sorting out problems caused in a sketchily supervised lunchbreak.

The supervision itself does not, of course, have to be stern and Draconian. Most of the time it is enough simply for someone to be there. Additionally, though, teachers will probably want to use these times for chatting to children, either individually or in groups.

Action checklist

1. Never forget bullying. Don't believe that it's not happening.
2. Constantly encourage a 'disclosing' ethos in class.
3. Open up other 'disclosing' channels – talk to cleaners, dinner supervisors about watching for bullying and listening to children.
4. Use role-play and drama in class to let children express and act out fears and tensions.
5. Look for potential victims.
6. Be vigilant on the playground and in corridors.
7. Visit quiet places unexpectedly.
8. Draw the attention of colleagues to supervision 'gaps'.
9. Take parental complaints seriously. Refer them upwards and keep following up.
10. If you can spare the time, run a 'safe' classroom at break and lunchtime – let children be with you if they want.

Whether or not extra supervision goes further and becomes structured activity is something a few schools have grappled with. The long lunchtime on the playground, for example, is so problematic at times that it might seem sensible to organize a variety of playground activities. A self-managing school, under local management, might well want to consider employing, among its lunchtime supervisors, one or more people who can act as a 'playleader'.

4
POOR SCHOOL ATTENDANCE

Most schools will have, in varying degree, a number of children whose rate of absence from school is significant enough to have a measurable effect on their learning. Very occasionally the reason for this is that the child is struggling against a long-term medical condition. Many teachers can tell of children and parents whose courage in the face of illness, measured in determination to attend school as much as possible, has been an inspiration to the whole community. Most local authorities have arrangements to keep such children in touch with education during their absences and, in any case, a caring and supportive school will make its own arrangements for work to go to and from the home or hospital.

Much more common, alas, is the child whose attendance record is patchy simply because his or her parents are too ready to keep him or her away from school. There are one or two surface reasons for this. One is an exaggerated response to colds, tummy-aches and the like. Another is a domestic scale of priorities that places helping with a problem at home above the importance of going to school.

I say 'surface' reasons here because the underlying pressures are often extremely deep seated and obscure. Teachers are, for example, slow to grasp that the *real* reason a child is being kept at home a lot is because one of the parents – usually the mother – has an inner need to have the child with her. Going one step further and considering the reasons for *this* probably takes us beyond our brief as teachers. A mother may, for example, have lost a child at some point, and be subconsciously reluctant to let a remaining one out of her sight. These are deep waters best plumbed by others, but the knowledge that the currents are flowing can help to explain some otherwise puzzling cases of poor attendance.

Part of the teacher's classroom management job is to keep an eye on each child's attendance and to refer onwards any worrying cases. Things to take notice of are the following:

- An unexplained absence that goes on longer than two or three days. The school should find out, in such a case, what the reason for the absence is.
- High frequency of short absences – a couple of days off every fortnight or so. Again, this is something for the school to look into.
- A noticeable 'pattern' of absences – every Wednesday afternoon, for example. Sometimes this turns out to be connected with something that happens in school at that time. Equally, though, the link may be with a regular happening at home.

In a well-run school, attendance queries will be picked up independently of the class teacher. The head, for example, may look through the registers every week, and in some areas the education welfare officer (EWO) also inspects registers. The class teacher, however, is the first line of defence. Should the head miss one 'register inspection' because of a meeting or illness, then a worrying case may not be picked up for another week.

Attendance, particularly when it is poor, is a common topic in interviews with parents. Often parents are defensive, professing considerable worry about the amount of time their child is losing. This worry, and the child's frequent illness, may be genuine, in which case there should be onward referral of the problem so that the head can either contact the family's GP or involve school health. Too often, though, the concern is a defensive sham. In this case the teacher's role is to point out, sympathetically but firmly, the importance of continuous school attendance. A comparison of their child's work with that of a regular attender, drawing attention to thin work folders and gaps in exercise books, often helps to bring the discussion to earth.

It is also important to probe for possible problems in school that are being masked by the child feigning illness or actually having psychosomatic tummy-aches. Worries about bullying, about changing for PE and games, fear of swimming, fear of riding a bus to the games field, passing worries about topics in maths, English or other subjects, fear of a particular teacher – these and a host of other things, some unbelievably obscure, can cause a child to be unwell on a particular school day. Deciding when to over-ride pathetic tears and when to give in is one of those difficult parenting tasks that nobody is trained for. It does help, though, if the teacher can be friendly and sympathetic enough for the parent to be frank about the problem. If the home–school relationship is good, a parent should be able to say, or write in a note, 'I really am not sure whether John is ill or not, so I've sent him in. If he turns out to be really poorly, you can get me at . . .' Obviously, such messages are better sent without the child's knowledge.

Truancy

When children stay away from school they are just 'absent'. If they stay away and their parents think they are in school it becomes 'truancy'. The first thing to recongize about truancy is that it is a serious business. I say this because there is a certain amount of cultural acceptance, even half-approval, of truancy. It conjures up a sort of *Beano* image of lively lads heading for the countryside with fishing-rods. 'We all used to wag off', is something that parents, especially fathers, will sometimes say when faced with the fact of their children having truanted.

The problem is quite simple really. A child who truants can be out and about, often in highly dangerous surroundings, for several hours each day, during which time each party – school and home – believe him or her to be safe. This, of course, is what makes truanting attractive to the child. There is a deadline – usually the normal time of arrival home from school – up to which absolute freedom beckons.

Just to counteract the image of the jolly anglers, it needs to be pointed out that children who play truant can, and do, get involved in any or all of the following:

- Theft from shops.
- Theft from, or of, cars.
- Playing near attractive but lethal farm, construction and industrial sites.
- Sexual games with older people that verge on, or become, criminal abuse.
- Glue-sniffing and other forms of substance abuse.

It is easy to say, of course, that a child who gets mixed up in these things may do them anyway in the evenings and at weekend, and that truancy is only a part of a bigger problem. This may be true, but the teacher has to tackle those bits of the problem that belong to him or her. And in any case, it seems reasonable to assume that truancy may be the route by which a relatively unscathed child may be introduced to a more worrying sub-culture.

Prevention of truancy

The most important strategy, as always, is prevention. A teacher ought to be running his or her class in such a way that truancy surfaces before too long. A child, especially in a primary school, who successfully stays away for a week without being caught is showing up a serious management failure.

The key is the register. In almost every school, at each session, the teacher marks the register, noting absences. Sometimes there is a lot going on in the classroom at this time – children are walking about getting their reading books, bringing dinner money up to the desk or just generally chatting to each other. It can be a good, relaxed moment in the day, cherished by the teacher and children alike, and it may be quite possible for the teacher, especially if he or she knows his or her class well, to mark the register accurately in the midst of what looks to the outside like subdued chaos.

On the whole, though, it is probably better if the children sit down and keep quiet while the register is marked, answering their names in the traditional way with 'Here' or 'Yes, Miss/Sir' or whatever is the school convention. The reason for this is that the ceremony establishes 'registration' as important, and subtly builds it up as a serious barrier the potential truant will have in mind when considering staying away.

Doing it this way also ensures accuracy. The register does not just have to be accurate – the teacher has to be inwardly convinced of its accuracy. This is to say that if the class has gone off swimming with another teacher, and the head rushes in to say, 'Is Jimmy Smith in school today?' then teacher must have no little frissons of doubt about whether he or she has marked the register correctly. The register is the basic document of school attendance and it assumes major importance in emergencies and in court cases about non-attendance.

Having marked the register accurately, the next thing is to remark to the class on absentees. This is done to help the class realize that their teacher is interested in whether they are there or not, and that he or she notices straight away any change in the pattern. 'I see John's away today. Anybody know what's the matter?' Not only will this often produce actual hard information, it also demonstrates genuine concern for the welfare of each child. Similarly, if a child is adding another day to a continuing absence, a concerned comment serves the dual purpose of showing interest and of letting potential truanters know that teacher notices.

Registration time is when children returning from legitimate absence bring notes for the teacher. It is a part of good class management to ensure that every absence is covered by a note from home. Many families are poor at sending notes in – for no other reason than the ordinary domestic disorganization that afflicts many of us. Sometimes, too, there is slight resentment that the word of the child is not going to be accepted. The only way round this is to hide behind the fact that it is school policy to demand a note from everyone, and to explain that any attempt to insist on notes from some families and not from others would be unfair and unworkable. Where a note is not forthcoming within a couple of days, the matter should be referred to the head, who will probably send out an inquiry or, in a really doubtful case, enlist the help of the EWO.

Often the message will be verbal – a parent will call in to the classroom, or will phone the school. When this happens, the message should be converted into a brief written memo by the teacher and added to the file of absence notes.

Responding to truancy

It does not, of course, end there. Each neatly inked zero in the register has to be tackled – however briefly – each day. The best way to think of it is to consider what would happen were the head to come in (as he or she should, from time to time) and ask, 'Why is John away?' The teacher's response might, of course, be 'Come on. It's only half past ten and he hasn't been away for weeks. I haven't done any real investigation and I do not intend to. The children say he's got a bad cough, and I've no reason to doubt them'.

On the other hand, John might be a pupil known to have truanted before, or to be someone whose general behaviour pattern gives cause for concern, in which case by 10.30 a.m. the teacher ought to have done something about his absence. Exactly what will depend on the school's own system, but at some point, very early in the day, John's absence should be notified to the head or the deputy. A few questions will usually provide some additional helpful information. Does he have brothers or sisters in school? Are they away? Questioning John's sister, though, if it is done at all, needs doing with care. She may be under enough pressure already and the last thing she wants is to feel that she is carrying responsibility for her brother. It is, too, the work of a moment to check whether John's known close friends are in school. If it turns out that he and a couple of cronies are suddenly away together, then the alarm bells need to ring.

Action beyond this point will usually be taken by the head or the deputy. Should they be unavailable, though, it is important not to wait too long – the key to stopping truancy from becoming a habit, or from spreading to other children, is to show that it is always picked up immediately. One seemingly obvious check is to ring the absentee's home. This does need tact, however, especially if the teacher has had relationship difficulties with the parents. A parent whose attitude to school is already resentful is not going to feel very happy about being phoned to see if his or her son is playing truant when he is actually lying upstairs covered in spots. And as likely as not, life being as it is, at the moment the phone goes he will be shouting for a drink of water, the baby will be crying and the washing-machine leaking all over the floor. One way round this is to get the secretary to ring on some administrative pretext. 'I'm just checking the registers. John's away today. Sorry to bother you, but if he's going to be away all week, could somebody bring his trip money in?' (A teacher and a good secretary will always think of something. It might still sound a bit lame and petty, but better safe than sorry.)

If the check call does reveal that John is truanting, the best thing to do is to ask the parent, first, to think of any obvious places he might be, and then to come to school to see the head.

At this point the EWO needs to be informed. Similarly, if phone contact cannot be made with John's home, the next step is to involve the EWO. The secretary will know how to do this, but it is worth remembering that if the EWO cannot be contacted – and they do spend a lot of time out and about – he or she will have a chief in an office who can be consulted. 'Hello, I'm Jane Smith from Smith Street Primary. The head and the deputy are both at the Civic Hall sorting out the school concert, the secretary's off ill, and I've got this problem.'

Any truanting incident, however short lived or apparently out of character, calls for serious home–school consultation. It is very likely, however, that there will be no obvious reason for it. A child questioned about playing truant, either by teacher or parent, will commonly – perhaps usually – show no desire to unload his or her troubles. As often as not he or she will say – and it will probably be true – that he or she did not really know why he or she did it. In many cases, too, this will be all there is to find out. Many a child is likely to join in a last minute group decision not to go to school but to branch off and go to the park instead. Many a teacher – indeed, many an adult in any sort of job – has felt like doing the same, and a proportion of people go ahead and do it. To that extent, occasional truancy can be seen as an eminently sensible reaction to the pressure of daily routine rather than as something deviant and worrying. The danger such action poses to children, though, has to be taken seriously, and it is this that places on teachers the duty of taking a kill-joy attitude. For such children, the certainty of detection is the best deterrent, and actually being caught is the best cure. The talk with the parents ought, first, to ascertain that they do understand the potential dangers – not all of them do at first – and then go on to suggest a strategy for early detection should it happen again. This usually means getting the parents to accept that they might be phoned or have a note pushed through the letter-box very early in the day.

For some children, though, the thing is not so simple. They stay away for reasons that are at the same time compelling and yet obscure – to the complete bewilderment, very often, of both teachers and parents. There are children who, day after day, will wander cold and rainswept streets or open spaces, or hide in dirty, disused buildings rather than face a warm, relaxed and happy school staffed by concerned and kindly folk. There may, of course, be hidden pressures to do with bullying or with fear of certain lessons, but such things by no means account for all the children who truant. In the last analysis there are cases that entirely defy all explanation. The children themselves, of course, will offer no help beyond a shrug of the shoulders or perhaps an enraged, 'I hate it here!' – forcing the conclusion that they do not themselves know what it is that causes this terrible feeling about school.

Action checklist

1. Be aware of attendance – know who is here and who is away.
2. Mark the register carefully – would you be confident of its accuracy if the fire brigade were using it to confirm that all your children were safe from a blazing school building?
3. Watch for absence patterns – of days, of friendship groups.
4. Let the class know that you are aware of attendance patterns.
5. Always refer on doubtful cases – never sit on your suspicion that a child is truanting.
6. Be sensitive in discussing absence with parents – all manner of family problems may be hidden.
7. At the same time, be firm if necessary – the child only has one stab at education, and in any case may be better off in a stable classroom atmosphere.
8. Be firm also in convincing parents of the dangers of truancy. Do not accept the 'I did it when I was a lad!' ploy. Most parents are aware of hazards, but some are not.
9. Where school problems are given as reasons for truancy, be accepting and prepared to investigate.
10. Do not, however, feel pressured and responsible. Hidden reasons for truancy or for school refusal are often well beyond the reach of individual teachers.

In the end, this is something for which the teacher and the family need support. There may be a case for special-needs referral, but in any case the school's own support mechanisms should be brought into play to help the teacher. In a case like this – as with so many other problems – the class teacher should not feel the burden pressing too heavily. It is important, first, that he or she does not assume personal responsibility for a child's truancy and, second, to remember that his or her job is to manage the class efficiently and with care. Part of this management task is that of referring intractable problems onward, continuing to share in the resultant procedures but without feeling threatened, remorseful or guilty.

5
PERSONALITY CLASH

Occasionally it seems that a teacher and a particular pupil do not seem to be able to hit it off together. There is, to use the cliché that appears on these occasions, 'a personality clash'. How does this problem surface? There are various ways. A parent may, at parents' evening, for example, suggest the personality clash as a counter to the teacher's opinion that a pupil is not trying very hard. 'I'm sorry to say it, but she just doesn't seem to like you very much.'

Occasionally the teacher may make the suggestion – to the head, perhaps, when discussing a child's progress: 'I'm sorry, but I just can't seem to like him. He's not a very lovable child after all.' Or, as an extension of this, 'I like most children. It's not often you hear me say I don't like somebody, but Jimmy Smith – I'm sorry, but there's just something about him'.

There are two levels of response to this. Clearly, if the state of affairs is exactly as explained – that the teacher and child for some reason just rub each other up the wrong way – then consideration has to be given to moving the child to another class. Before that point is reached, however, the problem has to be looked at in a bit more detail.

If the parent who suggests that his or her child dislikes the teacher is questioned a bit more – 'What exactly does she not like about life in my classroom?' – the most usual reason given is that she is 'fed up of being picked on'. What has happened here is that the child, for whatever reason, feels that she is constantly being admonished and punished, often unfairly and certainly more frequently than other people in the class. Taking the analysis one more step further back, the reasons for this kind of perception are varied. One possibility, of course, is that it is true. All teachers need to be very self-analytical, all the time, about their treatment of children. It is much easier than anyone thinks to fall almost unconsciously into the habit of disproportionately noticing one child's misbehaviour. This is the phenomenon of 'labelling', yet again; its power in the pupil–teacher relationship cannot be over-estimated.

More usually, the teacher will want to counter with something like, 'If she behaved herself I wouldn't have to notice her'. By implication, the teacher feels that the child – and her parents – are asking for the child's misbehaviour to be unjustly ignored.

Quite clearly this is a classic manifestation of the vicious circle. Misbehaviour – correction – pupil resentment – more misbehaviour – the cycle can be entered at any point, and when it is running strongly downhill it will probably only be stopped by some dramatic event from which nobody will emerge with any advantage or credit.

Given that a child may dislike his or her teacher – for whatever reason, and with whatever justice – what do teachers do if they really do dislike one of their children? The answer to this is simply that teachers cannot – must not – get into this position. Disliking children is just not part of a teacher's job. When teachers feel it coming on, they just have to make redoubled efforts to compensate. Nothing can possibly be worse for a child than to feel that his or her teacher, with whom he or she does have to spend a great deal of time, harbours personal feelings against him or her.

The teacher's feelings

Some of the people who work in schools, alas, do not like children at all. This is a matter of common observation. Now clearly there is no law that says everyone has to like children – W. C. Fields was famous for his general vendetta against everyone under the age of about 19, and a club comedian I know gets a bigger laugh than you might think when he says, 'Now I want all the kids to come and sit together at the front here – because I've only got one hand-grenade'. Disliking children is one thing, though. Working in a school when you feel like this is quite another. There may be some excuse for ancillary staff – caretakers, cleaners, school-meals workers – because they may simply have to work wherever the opportunity presents itself. And, in fact, the devotion to children many such people display puts many a teacher to shame.

To my mind, however, there is no possible excuse for a teacher not liking children, because anybody who feels like that should surely go and do something else. Quite apart from anything else, there is the simple issue of sanity. Being a teacher is a hard and stressful job in itself. The major – perhaps the only – compensations are to be found in enjoying the company of children. Take that away and the job surely becomes entirely unbearable.

A teacher who dislikes children, therefore, is probably an unhappy teacher. This means that his or her classes get a double dose of aggravation – one by being the brunt of their teacher's general dislike, and another from the extra irritation that he or she feels from having to put up with their unamusing presence. The most fundamental question, therefore, any new or prospective teachers have to ask themselves is whether they actually like being with children. If they do not, then they had better think of another career.

If they do like them, however – and experience shows that the majority of new entrants to the profession do – then it follows that they must show this. It is too easy to go through the day frowning from concentration and from worry about getting through the work. A class needs care and attention from their teacher. They need him or her to sit with them, listening to their chatter and putting in some gossip of his or her own. They need to see their teacher smiling; they need to know that he or she will hold their hands walking down to assembly, and bring his or her pet cat in for them to see.

What is important, though, is that they all share this need. Any class contains lots of very personable and pushy children who will, given half a chance, gather round the teacher's desk to listen and talk. In the background, however, are others, apparently unconcerned but actually as much – or more – in need of attention. Children have a right to education. Even more importantly, though, they have a right to attention, affection and love. The teacher's job is to reach out to each and every child in his or her care, impartially and regardless of personal preference. There does not exist the luxury of choosing where to place affection.

This needs to be said because teachers, as the saying goes, are human and fall naturally into human ways of behaving. It is too easy to smile at one child and frown at another; to welcome one and to ignore another. It is even easier to give similar messages in much more subtle ways. Classroom observers – teaching-practice tutors, heads, advisers – sometimes spend time measuring the amount of attention a teacher gives to each child in the class. When the teacher is unaware that this is happening, the results are invariably illuminating – they always, without fail, show that there is a fundamental unfairness in the way that most teachers operate – to put it simply, some children get more than their fair share of attention. Faced with this, a teacher will protest – the observer, surely, has missed the obvious point that some children actually *need* more attention than others. Closer analysis, however, always shows that even when this is taken into account, the unfairness is still there. What is happening is that some children are favoured when hands go up to answer, some are favoured when the teacher moves round the room, some are favoured when children wish to come out to the teacher's desk. There are other, subtler, favourings connected with smiles, words and praise, and even subtler ones connected with such things as posture.

Who gets the extra attention? The simplest analysis might suggest that the 'little girls in white' factor is at work here – the favouring of attractive, smiling and well-dressed children. Certainly this is a danger. The teacher may, after all, have been such a child. It is by no means always as simple as that, however. Just as you might find a teacher who 'likes' girls in clean blouses, so you will always find another who has a 'soft spot for the lads' – this meaning, often, that a certain amount of cheerful cheek from a certain kind of boy may well provoke amusement rather than outrage. Personal factors come into all this – who knows why one person is attracted to another? Generalizations seem impossible.

What is important, however, is for the teacher to be aware of the problem and to try hard to compensate for it. That this is not easy is obvious. What can help is to regard it not just as a matter of feelings and attitudes, but of technique and class management. When the teacher is having a question-and-answer session with the class, for instance, distributing attention round the answerers, and encouraging those who do not raise their hands, is a matter of alertness and technique. 'Put your hand down if you've already suggested something.' 'Now, who hasn't given me an idea at all yet? John, what about you?'

Positive reinforcement

Similarly, in sessions like this, the ability to run them in an encouraging way, so that children are not afraid to volunteer something, is again a matter of technique. The most basic thing is to be generally accepting of what children say. Children are easily discouraged if they suddenly realize that what they have said is 'wrong' or, worse, ridiculous. Some teachers have a legendary tendency to accept as 'right' anything at all that children say. 'Now, boys and girls, who can tell me the name of this prehistoric flying reptile? Margaret?'

'Pigeon, Miss.'

'Very good, Mary, you're on the right lines. A pigeon does fly, but if you look closely . . .'

At times this teeters on the verge of absurdity, but what the teacher is doing here is rewarding the child not for getting the right answer but for having a go and being involved. This often shows in teacher's response when other children laugh at a classmate's answer. 'I don't think it's funny! At least Margaret put her hand up and tried. It shows she's listening, which is more than can be said for some of the ones who're making fun of her. Never mind Margaret, *I* liked your answer, because it showed you were trying hard. Well done!'

It is important not to make too much of a meal of this – a teacher may well end up knowing his or her class so well that he or she can afford a little ridicule of his or her own, for example, and gushing acceptance of everything the child has to offer can end up seeming a trifle wearing. Nevertheless, a teacher has, perforce, to be relentlessly positive to all of the children in his or her charge.

Favouritism

To reinforce this, consider the opposite side of the coin – the teacher who has developed, only half-consciously, the habit of being negative and rejecting to one particular child or group in the class. How often do you hear, for example, a teacher say something like, 'John Smith? I might have known it would be you again!' Or 'I want four really reliable children to do this job – not you John Smith?' Or 'I'm telling you now, John Smith, if you don't behave during the concert, you'll be straight up to Mr Smithers when we get back to class.' And in reinforcement of this, how often do you hear, directed at other children, 'I'm really surprised at you, Mark Jones. It's not like you to behave in this way!' (The clear implication being that there are other children in the class who are expected to misbehave.) There are actions, too that speak just as loud as words. How often does a teacher move two children apart from each other at the start of assembly or some special event, the clear message being that he or she does not trust them to behave themselves if they are together?

The point about all this is that although most – perhaps all – teachers would, and do, instantly and hotly deny any accusation of favouritism, many of the same teachers should easily recognize some of the little events I have described. Favouritism, together with its mirror image, victimization, is considerably more insidious and pervasive than teachers would care to admit even to themselves. The first step towards avoiding it, though, is to admit the possibility of its existence, and many teachers find this very difficult.

What is necessary, then, is for the teacher who is accused – by parent or child – of victimization or favouritism to at least consider whether, however inadvertantly or subliminally, he or she has been unduly negative in his or her dealings with one child or group.

Action checklist

1. Don't assume that you are even-handed with praise and blame: few teachers are. Recognizing the problem is the first step to dealing with it.
2. Get a colleague to observe, paying particular attention to your distribution of attention around the room.
3. Do you, hand on heart, dislike any of the children in your class? Start by realizing that you cannot do this. You must totally and unconditionally accept all your pupils as they are.
4. Do you *work* at relationships with children? You cannot always just 'be yourself'; sometimes you have to overcome all manner of negative feelings, from a simple hangover to bitter disappointment at being passed over for promotion.

6
SELF-IMAGE

A head spoke to me scathingly about a fellow head in the town where he worked – they had been at a meeting together. 'Not once did he mention children! It was all about money and marketing and juggling resources.' Implicit in what he said was his belief that the greatest mistake any educator can make is to lose sight of children. The greatest teachers are remembered not for their grasp of management principles or for their mastery of curriculum theory but for their love of children and awareness of their needs.

Following from that is the necessity to realize that the greatest need of every child is for a good self-image. A child who feels good about him or herself is a child who is equipped for learning. Thus, inexorably, the teacher's greatest challenge is that of raising and maintaining the level of self-esteem of the pupils. This might seem fairly obvious. A moment's observation, though, shows how often teachers fail to consider the need for pupils to have good feelings about themselves. Consider the way that teachers put children down by belittling them, ignoring them, failing to take them seriously and curtly dismissing them.

Much of the strategy involved in helping children with problems is concerned with improving self-image. The idea is to help the individual child feel valued. The term 'self-image' is much used as such psycho-sociological labels tend to be – but it expresses concisely how important it is that each child should feel good about him or herself. Not that it is any different for adults. Let a teacher have one bad day of feeling unappreciated by authority, belittled by a parent and scorned by a group of pupils and he or she will not be in the right frame of mind to act like a cheerful, well-adjusted member of the family group when he or she gets home. Similarly, the pupil who arrives in school having been belittled at home, or made to feel that he or she is unloved and unwanted, is not best equipped to behave like the little girls who, in the American phrase, 'Wear white dresses and jump rope'. Such children are probably not going to get through the day without trouble unless they get a boost of some kind in class. The pity of it is that so often exactly the opposite happens – the child, perhaps already carrying a trouble-making label – arrives in school in a black mood and by 9.05 a.m. standing at the head's door having been caught pushing or fighting on the playground or on the way into school. He or she then gets a telling-off that sets the tone of his or her response for the rest of the day.

How can the teacher help the children in the class to feel good about themselves? Here are some random ideas:

- Be in the classroom before they arrive in the morning. Look busy – putting up work or arranging flowers. This helps the children to feel that you care about their room and being with them. The opposite approach is to arrive late, looking grumpy and disorganized.
- As the children arrive, greet each one by name, with a smile.
- Have an arrival routine that gets each child sitting down doing something quietly. Do not start the day by having to yell instructions and admonish children who are not listening.
- When all the children are in and sitting quietly, have some time talking with them as a class – smile and be pleasant.
- Do not do the register by numbers – use names, and try to look and smile at each child as the name is called.
- Children have to be told off, and there is no need to be 'soft' or lenient. It is vital, though, for the child to understand that it is the *behaviour* that is unacceptable, and that the child him or herself is still valued and respected.
- Thus, do not 'name call' children in a disrespectful or demeaning way ('Stupid boy!' 'You're a disgrace to the school!') Name the *behaviour*, not the child.
- When the telling off is finished, agree on the next step with the child – if possible, get the child to suggest what might be done to make amends.
- Avoid fraught scenes. If a child is 'steamed up' and indignant, make an

excuse to leave him or her alone for a few minutes – 'Sit here, I've got to go and get some books'. This will give a bit of breathing space for him or her – and you – to calm down.

- The key to all of this, really, is to be *accepting* of children – to take them as they are, unconditionally. This is not, to say the least, easy, but it should be the aim.

Part III: Home and School

A retired head, replete with professional folk-tales, once told me of the time he had visited a local grammar school. He had walked in through the imposing oak front door only to be accosted by the head master and brusquely told to use the side entrance in future. The visitor apologized and introduced himself, whereupon the atmosphere changed and the grammar-school head said, 'I'm sorry, I quite thought you were a parent!'

Such stories are common and reinforce the received view that once upon a time schools were aloof from parents. The same received view assumes that things are much better now. There is probably a great deal of truth in all of this. The fact remains, though, that we are dealing here with generalizations – that there were pre-war schools in which parents were welcomed as friends; and that there are schools today where the reality of home–school relations falls short of the brochure policy.

This being so, it needs to be restated constantly that good understanding between parents and teachers is not just a sensible idea but actually produces measurable improvements in learning. A home–school approach to reading, for example, improves progress, and similar co-operation on disciplinary matters reduces confrontation and misunderstanding. At the heart of the home–school relationship is the class teacher. Increasingly, class teachers are visited by parents either formally by appointment or informally as children are being delivered to or collected from school. Teachers have to learn how to cope with this without feeling either threatened or inadequate, and have to remain convinced that even when things become difficult – as they assuredly will from time to time – the contacts have to be kept alive.

7
CONTACT WITH PARENTS

Teachers have always had an ambivalent relationship with the parents of their pupils. The problem is caused by a difference of focus – teachers see their pupils as a class, a kind of organic whole like a swarm of bees or a flock of starlings. This is not to say that they have no concern for the individual for they have, but it is certainly true that a strong part of their concern is with the individual's relationship with, and effect on, the rest of the class. Much of the exasperation a teacher feels for a difficult child arises because he or she is being distracted from the rest of the class.

Parents, on the other hand, tend to see only their own children, and while they will usually pay at least lip-service to the relationship between their child and others, their focus is very strongly on their own child.

Thus it is true to say that the nature of schooling and of classroom life carries within it a constant potential for conflict between parent and teacher. The whole can be visualized something like this – in the centre is the teacher. Around him or her are thirty children, all relating to the teacher and to one another. And all around the edge are thirty sets of parents, each relating strongly to one child out of the thirty – monitoring, as it were, the way that their own child is treated by the teacher and by other children.

There are all sorts of extra complications, of course. All parents, for example, are very slow to see faults in their own children. The bonds of love and protectiveness are immensely strong. And just to make all that more difficult, there is the unreliability of the mechanism by which parents monitor what goes on in school. On the whole the only regular way a parent can find out what happened on any particular day is by asking his or her own child about it. That this can be a flawed channel of communication is probably a wild understatement.

What does all this lead to? Let us consider some examples.

Parent–teacher horror story 1 – Gurdip   Gurdip is a very lively boy of 10, quite bright and enormously active. Unfortunately his high rate of activity leads him to get into arguments and fights with the other children. If he is not carefully watched he will goad other children into losing their tempers, or will surreptitiously poke or kick them until they retaliate. He is also likely to walk about the classroom causing disruption by 'borrowing' pens, rubbers and rulers. Often the first sign of trouble is an angry shout not from Gurdip but from somebody else. He is very adept at manipulating classroom life – he knows who will cry if he calls them names; he knows who will be intimidated by threats.

The problem is that Gurdip's teacher has never managed to convince his parents that there is any real difficulty with him. They see him as a 'normal' boy, with mischievous boyish traits, who is continually being put down by his teachers and unjustly complained about by the more feeble children of more feeble parents. If only his teachers were not so quick to jump on his every foible; if only the head were not so quick to believe the whingeing of other children; if only that awful Johnny Foster could be moved to another class. Gurdip, after all, is a perfectly behaved boy at home – he goes shopping for his grandma. Are other children being picked on in this way? Are other parents being called in to discuss the behaviour of their children? What has been done about Gurdip's torn coat?

Parent–teacher horror story 2 – Rebecca   Rebecca is an 11-year-old girl. She is intelligent, amusing and popular with the rest of the class. Her parents, however, know all about the horrors of adolescence, and are on the watch for anything that heralds the onset of delinquency. Rebecca is being a problem at home. She leaves her room untidy. She has to be told to clean her teeth. The other week she brought a very unsuitable friend home to tea. We have very high standards in our house. Tell me, are we wrong to have high standards? We will not let Rebecca walk into town on her own. She cannot do PE if it is raining. Can she sit with someone else, please, because we once heard Jane Oswestry swear. Rebecca came home with a very unsuitable book called *The Machine Gunners*. It has swear words in it. This is a church school, is it not? Are we wrong to have higher standards than anyone else? Our only thought is to do our best for our children.

Parent–teacher horror story 3 – Kevin   Kevin is 7. He is finding it very difficult to learn to read and has actually made hardly any progress since he started schools. He is becoming discouraged, and his behaviour is starting to deteriorate. The school wants him assessed under the special-needs legislation. Their own judgement is that he will not cope with mainstream schooling. Kevin's parents have a deep-seated aversion to the whole notion of psychology, special help and special schooling.

He's not going to one of those schools. Our Kevin doesn't need any psychologist. He'll pick up when he gets into the next class. What about that lad on 'Brookside'? He had dyslexia. Has our Kevin got dyslexia? Have you found out whether he's got it or not? He can read at home. He read to me last night. He's just unhappy at school. He's not going to make any progress while he's unhappy, is he? Can't he have some homework to help him catch up? His sister's a lovely reader and she's only 5. I keep telling him she'll be leaving him behind if he doesn't buck up.

Anyone who works in a school could go on and on adding to a list like this. I include these three examples simply to show the nature of the home–school relationship. It should not be assumed that they are intended to show how silly some parents can be. There are sillinesses in them, certainly, but they are usually born of genuine anxiety, and what is important is that teachers should address the anxiety rather than scoff at the silliness. Teachers need also to bear in mind the need to be self-critical. It is too easy to write off parental opinions, to weigh them against professional judgements and find them wanting.

Look, for instance, at some of the things in these three horror stories. Gurdip's dad thinks that teachers are too quick to jump on the boy. Hand on heart, are parents always wrong when they say this? One of the biggest problems in classroom relationships is that of 'labelling'. Once a child gets a name for being badly behaved, it is all too easy to keep piling on the agony. Here is a story to illustrate what I mean.

As a supply teacher, I spent a morning with a class of 12-year-olds. One boy in the class was generally reckoned to be disruptive and difficult. However, he was well behaved all morning, particularly enjoying a long reading I gave from Roald Dahl's autobiography. Towards the end of the morning, I said, 'There's only twenty minutes left. You've all done well up to now, so you can either read quietly or finish any outstanding work'. The 'disruptive' boy chose to read. He kept this up for a bit and then, with only ten minutes to go, he closed his book, leaned back and started abstractedly drumming with two pencils. I made a deliberate decision to ignore this – he had, after all, done well, and was within an ace of reaching lunchtime without being in any trouble at all. At this point the year leader came in to see the class, spotted the boy doing nothing, tore him off a terrific strip and set him to do some punitive work.

School life, it seems to me, can be like that. A class teacher who leaves his or her room for a few seconds and then returns may find him or herself homing straight in on one particular child who is playing about or out of his or her place. 'You again! I can't leave you for two minutes!' The teacher would hotly deny that the child was being 'picked on', but at the very least there may be room for debate. A teacher might well consider the way that his or her eyes are irresistibly drawn to one or two particular children – in assembly, say, or on the school trip. Are these one or two really the only ones misbehaving? Or is it just that everyone expects them to get into trouble?

Then there is Rebecca. Is her dad really as neurotic as he sounds? Or is part of the problem that Rebecca is manipulating the situation a bit? Did her dad find the swear words in the reading book by chance, or did she help things on a bit? Does she take all her friends home, or just those most likely to shock her parents?

And what about Kevin? How would any teacher feel, for instance, were he or she to be called in and told that his or her child ought to see a psychologist? And did the teacher listen when Kevin's mum said he seemed to be able to read at home? Some children behave exactly thus, for a variety of reasons. It is at least worth looking into. As to dyslexia, what does the teacher think about this? For some teachers the word itself is a turn-off to the extent that they are likely to stop communicating with a parent who insists on using it. This is not, to say the least, helpful.

All children are different, all families are different and all schools and classrooms are different. Nevertheless, each of these stories is, in its own way, typical of the way parent–teacher relationships can break down almost before anyone can build them up. Each story demonstrates the difference of perspective parents and teachers respectively bring to the business of looking after their children. What is important is that teachers do not fall into the trap of assuming that their own perspective is always the right one. It is too easy to get angry with Gurdip's parents, to grit the teeth and ignore Rebecca's and to patronize Kevin's. What the teacher ought to bear in mind instead is that the fact of these parents coming to school at all shows they are concerned. Their concern deserves proper consideration.

Calling parents in

In many schools, asking parents into school is an early response whenever a child starts to cause worry. Thus parents may be called in when there is a series of 'naughty' incidents; when there is a single serious flouting of rules; when there is a developing problem with class work; and when there is evident unhappiness or any other significant change of personality or behaviour. In a school that works like this, teachers will commonly initiate the parental contact, perhaps by going to the head and asking for a child's parents to be called in. Sometimes, though not often, individual teachers may be in the habit of asking parents in without necessarily involving or informing the head. It is not easy to accept this as good practice – telling or asking the head is simple enough, and ought to be done whatever habits other teachers have fallen into.

It is important that a teacher should have a thought-out reason for initiating a meeting of this kind. It is not wise, for example, for a teacher to go to the head, red in the face after an emotionally bruising and perhaps humiliating encounter with a disruptive child and demand to see the parents, as if the very act of asking constituted in some way a kind of punishment for the child or an easing of stress for the teacher.

So what are the reasons for calling in parents? The fundamental one, I suppose, has to do simply with communication. We saw earlier that parents only have limited and flawed access to information about what goes on in school when they are not there. When a child is having a difficult and unhappy time, therefore, and is presumably taking unhappy messages home, it is politic, if nothing else, to set up a more direct channel of contact. It is also important for parents to have the opportunity of telling school of their own worries. Then, building on the shared experience, it may well be possible to work out a home–school strategy for dealing with the problem.

The flaw with this, fairly conventional, approach, is that parents are only 'called in' when there is a problem. As a result, whatever the school's view of what is going on, parents invariably regard the summons to school as a harbinger of trouble. They are likely, as a result, either to be on the defensive or ready to come out fighting in a counter attack. In the ideal world, communication between parents and teachers would be so good that there would rarely be the need to send a letter home asking for a special interview. Some schools approach the ideal, but they are exceptional, and there is the age-old principle to be considered that the parents you want to see are the ones who attend school most rarely.

Preparing to meet parents

The teacher who decides to see the parents of a child with a problem, or who is involved by the head in such contact, needs to prepare him or herself very carefully for the meeting. Gurdip's father, for example, may well take the line that the whole business is trivial, and when he asks for examples of his child's wrong-doing he is not going to be happy if the answers are vague. Behavioural psychologists talk about 'fuzzies' – 'He's always being aggressive'. 'He interferes with other children's work all the time' – and demand that all such judgements be made in terms of specific behaviours at specific times and dates. The same sort of rule could well apply in talking to parents. When Gurdip's dad says, 'Go on, then, what's he been doing wrong?' It will simply not be enough to say, 'He misbehaves in class', or 'He messes about all the time'.

The best way to prepare, of course, is to keep a diary for a time, noting down exact descriptions of problem behaviour, with dates and times. Examples of work – that may tie up with days when there have been behaviour problems – will also help.

It all needs very careful handling, though. Precise recording can be counter-productive if Gurdip's father sees it all as 'keeping a dossier on my son'. It is not unknown, either, for a parent to make a careful note of all the reported incidents, go back and discuss them with the child and then return to shoot them down one at a time – 'Then there was the shoe thrown out of the window. What happened was that the lad threw his own shoe out of the window and blamed Gurdip for it. Gurdip is quite sure of this and I believe him . . .'

This sort of difficulty arises when parents and teachers see themselves as adversaries – courtroom rivals, as it were. This is a common and sad state of affairs. It has its roots, perhaps, in the bad experience of schooling many adults have, and in the aloofness practised by many schools and teachers in the past.

What it all calls for is immense humility and patience on the part of the teacher. There is no future, it seems to me, in a teacher accepting the adversarial model. An interview with parents must be a continuous process of self-questioning, listening and, perhaps, of turning the other cheek. When combative approaches are made they should be turned aside.

With all this in mind, let us look a bit more closely at parent–teacher contact, using and building on the story of Gurdip. He is a 'naughty boy', a constant focus of the teacher's attention. She does not lie awake thinking about him – on the whole she can cope, and she has had far more disruptive pupils in her class. He is cheerful, generally pleasant in manner, and capable of excellent work. So what – and this is what his dad asks – is the problem? The problem is that Gurdip hates to sit still, and also gets a kick out of causing minor explosions and disputes in class. When the class is lined up to go down the corridor to assembly he is quite likely to pinch or kick the person ahead of him, especially if he knows that this will provoke a loud screech or an instant loss of temper from the victim. Alternatively, he may wait until he is walking into assembly and walk across the toes of several of the people already there. Other children in the school, knowing Gurdip's preferences, may single him out for being tripped up or pinched in turn. In class he will leave his place on the flimsiest of excuses, and will probably, while he is walking around, pocket somebody's pen – not with the intention of stealing it, but because it will cause a good row. Out in the playground he likes to run up behind people and push them, or slap them about the head as he passes by. Some children see him coming and avoid him. Others see red and pursue him to wreak vengeance. As a result he is quite often involved in fairly serious fights that have arisen from incidents he sees as utterly trivial. Sometimes the fights end up being between second and third parties. Gurdip having faded away into the background when it all started to look nasty.

The teacher, as a professional, knows all sorts of strategies for dealing with this. She wants to reward Gurdip when he sits still and works; she wants to build on his strengths by giving him responsibilities and special projects connected with his interests. She siezes on his classroom successes and makes as much capital from them as possible. She keeps vigilant and defuses incidents by organizing her 'lining up' in such a way that Gurdip is not given the opportunity for pinching and kicking. It is all extremely wearing, however, and she feels that at the very least she would like Gurdip's parents to know what is happening, and perhaps would like their co-operation in running some kind of helpful programme. Perhaps he can bring home a daily report, or one of those behavioural reinforcement charts where he has to colour in a spot on a dinosaur when he has sat still for thirty minutes. Whatever the outcome, however, she feels that the meeting has to take place.

In preparation for the meeting, and also as part of her general recording, she keeps a detailed diary for a week, noting down every single 'problem' incident in which Gurdip is involved. She also keeps a check on his work, noting days when he has done little or no work either because he has been wandering about the room or because he has been in some sort of trouble that has kept him out of the class seeing the head or the deputy. She also finds examples of good work, and of work that was obviously going to be good but that never got finished. Armed with all this, she welcomes Gurdip's mother and father to the classroom one evening after school.

It is not, to say the least, an easy interview. The teacher has thought long about how to start the talk off in a reasonable, non-combative style. 'Gurdip's not having an easy time in school at the moment', she decides to say. 'I thought we should talk about it, and I wonder first if you have any views about what is going on, and whether you have picked up anything from him?'

Afterwards she wondered if this was the right opening – it certainly seemed reasonable enough. What happened, though, was that Gurdip's father jumped straight in and said, 'He's really unhappy at school because, quite frankly, he's being victimized. Day after day he comes home saying he's been in trouble for this or that. It's always Gurdip and he's getting really discouraged and fed up. It's as if he can't move a muscle without getting jumped on. It's getting as he doesn't want to come to school. He didn't have any of this trouble when he was in the infants school'.

The teacher sat quietly for a few moments. The notion of Gurdip as 'unhappy' at school seemed quite bizarre to her, for he always bounces cheerfully in, and his antics during the day never seem to be in the slightest way accompanied by misery. The teacher was also very sceptical about his claim that there were not problems in the infants school. His record shows very clearly to the contrary, and indicates that similar meetings took place there.

'I'm surprised you say he's unhappy. He never looks unhappy at school, and he's never away.'

'Well, he is unhappy. He comes in with a face as long as a fiddle.'

The teacher decided at this point that Gurdip is quite deliberately enlisting the support of his parents against the school. This he is doing, first, by telling his own, heavily censored, version of events and, second, by stopping at his front door to adjust his face before going in. Father, at this point, fires another very commonly used weapon:

'I've talked to all his friends, and they say he gets picked on. I have them all for football training, and I hear what's going on in this school.'

This is a powerful ploy, used more often than anyone might think. It hits a young teacher like a punch in the stomach, because it immediately conjures up the image of a whole gang of his or her loyal and friendly pupils sitting around in a football changing-room talking up their feelings and attitudes and, in the process, tearing their teacher to shreds. A sports teacher faced with this would recognize what was going on and would immediately silence everyone. Gurdip's dad has no such professional qualms, and drinks it all in. The boys like him and are more ready to outdo each other with gossip. 'She shouts at him for nothing every day. There was that fight with Jim. Gurdip got sent to the head, but Jim never did. And the dinner ladies are always on at Gurdip.'

'The dinner ladies are always on at Gurdip,' said Gurdip's dad, cutting across the silence. 'What chance has the lad got? All you need is to show him some respect.'

At this point, the teacher decided that the time had come to be firm and frank.

'I'm not saying that Gurdip is the worst-behaved child in the school. I'm not suggesting that he is the only one who ever gets told off. What I am asking is that you believe me when I say there is something to worry about.'

The father went to say something in reply, but this time he was silenced by his wife. 'Listen a minute. You know as well as I do he isn't perfect. Listen to the teacher.'

The teacher went on, 'You've shown interest by coming in today. I'm wondering if you would agree to coming in at the same time every week, just to talk about what has happened during the week and how we all feel about it. It will give you the chance to bring up anything that's worrying you, and we can go over the diary I keep about Gurdip. We can talk face to face and try to keep things straight. We're all interested in the same thing, after all, which is Gurdip's welfare'.

The father shrugged his shoulders at this. 'Can't do any harm. We've always been willing to co-operate with school. I won't be able to come in of course, because I'm far too busy at work. The wife will come, though, and she'll keep me in touch.'

Teacher wasn't going to take this lying down. 'I know it's a problem getting off work, but it would be really nice if you could both come whenever you can, or perhaps you could take it in turns.'

She was fighting a losing battle here, however, and in the end had to accept that Gurdip's mother was going to be making the main contact. Father, it seemed, would only be appearing if there were a real emergency.

The point about this particular kind of parent–teacher discussion is that in the end there is no absolute need for both sides to come to total agreement amid the slapping of backs and the shaking of hands. What happens is that the teacher gropes for some level of acceptance, however shallow, and then sets up a programme of regular visits. Most parents will go along with – or at least find it difficult to turn down – an offer of regular contact, no matter how doubtful they feel about it.

This is not, of course, the end of the story. The regular visiting programme, for instance, has a built-in flaw in that it can result in a parent being informed of all manner of trivial incidents that, in the normal run of things, he or she would never hear about. The teacher is therefore faced with the decision – 'Do I tell everything, or I do seem to be dishonest by holding some things back because they are unimportant?' This needs care. On the one hand a concerned parent may want to hear everything – may indeed hear things from other sources. On the other, if the teacher starts with a long recitation of petty misdeeds – 'Then he laughed behind my back when I turned to the blackboard', the parent may feel that the process is all about blackening his or her son's character.

So far as possible, regular meetings of this kind need to be kept positive and forward-looking. They give an opportunity for parents to get things off their chests and, at the simplest level, they enable the two adults concerned to get to know one another. The important thing is to arrive at some sort of strategy – going through the weekly diary, perhaps, taking particular note of positive things.

It is important that nobody has high expectations of such meetings. If either parent or teacher go into them expecting that there will be an immediate and direct effect on the child, then there is a fair chance that they will be disappointed. At worst, what might happen is that either parent or teacher – or both – become disillusioned with it all and go dejectedly through the weekly routine in a purposeless way. If this starts to happen, relationships may end up being worse rather than better, because if the parent breaks off the meetings having decided that they are doing no good, then it is quite difficult to find any other way of moving forward. The teacher needs to be on the lookout for this kind of frustration because it can be well hidden – a parent may attend week by week, being polite but not over-friendly and all the time building up a head of steam that may suddenly burst out in a bout of recrimination. Alternatively, the other parent may appear on a separate occasion – at parents' evening, for example, and angrily denounce the meetings as a waste of time.

The worst example of this in my own experience was of a parent who attended regularly, week by week, for two terms to discuss her son's progress in school. Teacher felt at times that the meetings had been difficult – there was awkwardness between her and the parent, and a general feeling of unease. She clung, however, with the head's support, to the fact that the meetings were taking place and that the child could only benefit from this prolonged exchange of feelings and views. There was, to be sure, little change in the child's behaviour in class, which continued to be difficult and disruptive but, the teacher felt (and believed that the parent did too), that the position was at least being held, and that the right line to take was that contact was good of itself, could do no harm and ultimately may show more tangible results.

The mistake was to assume that the parent had the same perception. What she was experiencing – and this only came out when the explosion ultimately came – was a weekly visit she dreaded, at which her son's faults would yet again be recited to her to no obvious purpose. Other children knew that she was attending, so she felt exposed and singled out. Because she had no particular problem with the boy at home, she felt also that she was being dragged into a problem that was not really her concern.

At the end of the second term came the annual parents' evening. The boy's father came to this and together he and his wife saw the teacher and went over much the same ground as was being covered in the weekly meetings – a résumé of classroom and playground problems, an account of how the school was trying to deal with them and in implicit appeal to the parents to support the school's efforts and to continue the weekly visits. The father made no contribution to this discussion, but went instead to see the head, where he poured out a great deal of harboured resentment – the school was dragging out and blowing up out of all proportion what were essentially trivial incidents. All boys fight and get into mischief. Other parents are not called in week by week to account for the misdeeds of their children. The head, in other words, was confronted with the appalling realization that for the whole of the two terms that the parent–teacher meetings had been taking place, the parents' perception of what was going on was wildly askew from what the school thought it was. The very next day the parents went to enrol their son at a different school. The class teacher, it ought to be said, was not entirely cast down by this turn of events.

So where does all this leave us? Most importantly, not under-estimating the nature of the gulf that can exist between teacher and parent, and realizing that this gulf may not be wished away simply because the teacher wants it or assumes it. Whatever careful explanations may be made, in parent–teacher meetings of the kind I have described, the agenda is being set by the school, and the school cannot assume that all parents will be enthusiastic. Parents may go along with the arrangements – because not to do so would seem impolite or churlish – but surface acceptance or co-operation may hide something entirely different. And it all, in the end, comes down to the difference of perception I described at the beginning of the chapter – between that of the teacher, whose view is in the end rather impersonal, professional and class-based, and that of the parent, whose view is emotional, individual and very self-centred. Neither view is wrong – both, indeed, are entirely natural. The important thing is to recognize the differences between them.

How to improve things? It is important to realize that the sequence of events here described is perhaps not typical. Regular weekly (or fortnightly) meetings between the teacher and parent, at the request of the school, can, and do serve excellent purposes. They can become relaxed, open, productive and well worth the effort. The school, furthermore, has every right to call them and should not be ashamed of setting the rules and agenda. It is all, surely, part of the teacher's job. The important thing is to manage the meetings, and their context, properly so that the content and the purposes are clear to everyone. A teacher embarking on a series of regular meetings ought perhaps to proceed along the following lines.

Make Sure the Agenda is Clear

'We have no magic ointment, Mrs Kaur. We might meet for a whole year and feel we're not getting anywhere. It's an act of faith. While we're talking we are at least in touch and trying to understand each other. What I want to do is go over Gurdip's progress during the week. I will tell you the good things he has done, and I will let you know about any problems. I may not tell you all the problems, because some are going to be trivial, the sort of thing that any child might do. I will show you his work – and you can look yourself at any of his work for a few minutes before we get down to talking. For your part, I hope you will be able to tell me how he is at home; what he says about school; what things seem to make him happy or unhappy; and whether you ever see any of the same kind of problems that we have at school. Each week we will try to set some sort of small target – to read some pages to you; to draw a picture and bring it into school; or whatever we decide together. I really hope that you will speak up all the time when things are worrying you.'

Keep the Objectives Clear

This is not always easy – education, despite what some experts would have us belief, is not always a straightforward matter of defining aims and objectives and then heading towards them. This kind of meeting is a case in point. The very fact of its happening is a good and positive thing, and both aims and objectives may have to become clear as time goes on rather than be closely defined from the start. Perhaps the general aim should be agreed at a fairly modest level – 'What we want right now is to stop Gurdip's behaviour getting worse to the point where he is going to run into real trouble with authority. At the moment it is being contained, and ordinary class management techniques are sufficient. Let's see if together we can keep it like that'. Week-by-week objectives can then be derived from this. 'Let's look at lunchtimes this week, Mrs Kaur. Lunchtime is a particularly difficult time because of the amount of freedom that Gurdip has, among hundreds of children supervised by only a few dinner ladies. Let's think of ways of getting him through just one week of lunch hours without getting into trouble.' Doing this, of course, implies that the school will stick to the agenda. In other words, if the lunch hour has been singled out for special attention, it follows that Gurdip's mother did not ought to be confronted on her next visit with a list of misdemeanours that occurred at times other than in the lunch hour. Changing the rules in midstream is a sin of which schools are very commonly guilty!

Listen to what the Parent has to Say

Teachers are not always good listeners, which is a pity because the whole job is as much to do with listening as it is to do with holding forth. It is a serious mistake to regard these parent–teacher sessions as opportunities for uninterrupted discourse by the teacher. Few teachers will admit to seeing them in this way, but many will subconsciously operate as if they do. Teachers are often using this session, however marginally, as therapy for themselves – to talk things out, get them off their chests. A little self-questioning may result in a deliberate attempt to hold back a bit and to afford the parent the opportunity to do the same. If a parent offers what seems to be important information in a session like this – a significant change of behaviour, a worrying pattern of events or some change of circumstances in the home – the teacher ought to ask whether this is something that should be recorded. This leads to the next guideline.

Decide, and Agree with the Parent, what Sort of Record is to be Made of the Meetings

At the most basic level there will exist, on file, any exchange of letters that led to the setting up of the meetings. Properly, a brief note of each meeting should be added. It is sensible to agree this with the parent. One way is to start each meeting off by reading over the draft note of the previous one, and then agreeing the final version to add to the file. If the parent wants a copy, then he or she should have one. In any case, make sure that the note is factual and records the main points that were exchanged together with any decisions that were made about follow-up. A sample note might say the following.

'10 Dec. Meeting with Mrs Kaur. Showed her Gurdip's books; pointed out his good work in art and history. Told her about Gurdip's rough and tumble before school on Thursday. Agreed that she would reward Gurdip for his good classwork, and that she would try to make sure that he did not leave home quite so early in the morning. She pointed out this might be difficult as the whole family has to be out early in the morning. I said I would try to keep an eye on his arrival time and report back at the next meeting. Mrs Kaur said that she would give Gurdip the time to draw a sketch of a steam engine that her husband has in the shed, and make sure he brings it to school for us to see.'

The obvious advantage of a note like this is that it acts as a reminder to those who have to take some action and will also form, over a period of time, a pattern of events. The whole file of notes ought to be available at the meeting, and should be passed to the head at regular intervals.

Involve the Child

In a sense it is almost inevitable that this whole procedure will go on over the child's head – childhood often consists of watching decisions being made and having no hand in them. Nevertheless, when the teacher is counselling the child, he or she ought to refer to the parent–teacher discussions. What he or she must not do, though, is hold them over the child as a threat – 'I'll be seeing your mum on Friday my lad, and won't I have something to tell her?' This is unfair, and most unlikely to have any good effects. And if the parent hears about it, he or she will quite rightly object. It is not a good idea, though, to have the child routinely present at the meetings. The discussion needs to proceed without the inhibition that this would impose on both sides. There will, though be times when the child is called in by request of either parent or teacher, perhaps to receive some praise. On the whole, though, this ought not to happen too often – it always feels stilted and presents difficulties for all three parties.

Keep in Touch with the Head

As a matter of routine, every individual meeting ought to be reported verbally to the head, who will be able to suggest follow-up ideas and will also want to keep a hand on the proceedings anyway. The accumulating record, too, will go to the head at regular intervals. Whether or not he or she attends the meetings is a matter of judgement. There will be times when either parent or teacher asks for him or her to be there, and he or she may well invite him or herself to be present on occasion. If the relationship is difficult the head may want to provide support by being present; the problem is, however, that it is in exactly this kind of awkward setting that his or her presence might be most resented or misunderstood. The parent may feel that big guns are being brought to bear.

Action checklist

1. Be continuously aware that each child is the centre of one family's attention.
2. Try to get to know all 'your' parents – seek them out at school functions.
3. *Listen* to parents. Do not assume, outwardly or inwardly, a professionally superior manner.
4. Think how you feel when you see a senior doctor. Will 'your' parents feel like this when they see you?
5. Parents know a lot about their children. Be accepting of what they say.
6. Tell parents good news as well as bad – seek them out at functions to praise pieces of work or actions by their children.
7. Be frank. Really bad news about school progress should not come as an end-of-year shock.

8
PARENTS' EVENING

Most primary schools set aside an evening for interviews between parents and class teachers. There may be one a term, or one or two a year. It is not always an 'evening' – sometimes the time immediately after school is used; sometimes teachers are released one at a time to do their interviews in schooltime. Whatever the details of the arrangement, however, the principle is usually the same – each parent or set of parents is allocated a brief amount of time for a private talk with their child's teacher.

Many teachers approach parents' evening with a certain amount of trepidation, especially if the experience is a new one. In particular, they worry about encountering 'problem' parents – these being, usually, the parents of children who are difficult to cope with in class.

Preparing for a Parents' Evening

As with every other aspect of school life, the key to a satisfactory parents' evening is good preparation. What usually happens is that the parents are shown their children's books and other work, or are encouraged to browse freely through them in the classroom while waiting their turn. It follows that the teacher must make sure that he or she is familiar with anything that the parents may find there. It will take a long time, but the teacher must leaf through every exercise book and folder, making sure that marking is up to date, and trying to anticipate any questions about the content of the standard of the work. In addition, the teacher must have some notes, *aide-mémoires*, on every child. As part of the process of making these notes, he or she must speak to every other teacher who sees his or her children. If another teacher sees them for a substantial amount of time – if, for instance, as a probationer the teacher is released for in-service training for a day a week – then the other teacher should provide written notes of his or her own, which can be presented verbally to the parents coming from the other teacher.

The layout of the room for parents' evening is important. The teacher needs a desk because he or she will have notes and examples of work to hand. Teachers ought not, though, sit with their desks between themselves and visiting parents – it looks too reminiscent of other 'authority' encounters. Perhaps the best way is to sit half sideways by the desk, facing the parents in a way that does not put the desk in between as a barrier. Chairs (two) should be provided and, preferably, they should not be classroom chairs – if there is no system for providing 'good' chairs, a teacher could well simply borrow a couple from the staffroom or the library. Nobody is going to complain, and if they do it will be too late!

The teacher's attitude is important. He or she should dress in a business-like way – parents often 'dress up' for parents' evening, and for teacher to appear in slovenly gear is discourteous to them and will undoubtedly reinforce any prejudices that are already in the air. Teachers should never, by the way, believe that parents are in the least bit impressed or 'put at ease' by a teacher wearing informal clothes. On the contrary, parents expect their child's teacher to be someone who knows how to go shopping and how to dress suitably for an occasion. They will be too polite to comment openly on a teacher who turns up in denim, but they will think plenty and say lots to each other when they get home!

Also important is that parents are spoken to in a friendly and yet businesslike way. The teacher can get very tired as the evening wears on, but it is within the nature of the exercise that the last parents to visit should have the same attention and courtesy as the first. The teacher should rise to greet them and introduce him or herself by name. The opening gambit, always, is to ensure that the right child is going to be discussed – 'Let's see, you're. . .? And you've come to see me about. . .?' This can be embarrassing, especially if the parents have been into school before and could well expect to be recognized, but it is not half so embarrassing as starting to talk about the wrong child – something that happens far more often than anyone thinks!

The child's identity should be clearly confirmed with the full name as entered in the register. At the same time the relationship of the visitors to the child should be pinned down. The days when it was always mum and dad have long gone. Rather it is likely to be one parent and a current partner. The only way to check this is to ask, politely but openly and firmly. This might possibly be an invasion of privacy, but the teacher needs to know to whom he or she is talking. It is not unknown for there to be two or three visitors, neither parent being among them. Mother or father may have got into some sort of domestic crisis and sent along other members of the family. If this happens, the best thing is not to give too much information but to spend some time trying to fix an alternative appointment for the parent. Sometimes a parent will bring an interpreter, who may be the child him or herself or a brother or sister. Here, too, there has to be some care about confidentiality, although the fact that the parents have attended in circumstances that call for some effort and not a little courage, should be respected.

The biggest general problem about parents' evening is keeping to time. Ten minutes – which is a common allocation – is a very short time in which to have any kind of reasonable discussion about a child and his or her work, and yet it has to be kept to if people down the list are not to be kept waiting. It is extremely common for the parents' evening timetabling to break down. When this happens, queues build up and there is a good deal of resentment in the air. Often the class teacher, insulated in his or her room seeing parents individually, is unaware of the extent of the backlog or of the suppressed anger in the waiting queue. The headteacher may be going round looking at queues, and if the head comes into a room and says cheerfully, 'A few waiting, Miss Johnson!' then Miss Johnson had better not miss the hidden urgency in the message.

The only way to keep to time is to be really businesslike and keep control of the interview. A parents' evening is not an occasion for a relaxed chat or for in-depth counselling. It is for a brief exchange of information – five minutes putting facts about the child's progress; five minutes listening to the parent. If the parent wants to go on, then teacher has to step in and say, 'We will have to stop there. If you want to talk further about this, perhaps you can come in another time?' or if the problem surfacing seems both large and urgent, then the parents should be referred to the head. If necessary, the teacher can stand up and lead the parents from the room and down to the head or the secretary. Whatever happens, the schedule must not get completely out of joint. When it does, and parents are kept waiting, the professional image of teachers suffers enormously.

It is necessary, of course, to keep a brief note of each interview, making particularly sure to record any decision to see the parents again or to arrange for the parents to see somebody else in the school.

The traditional parents' evening is, in a sense, the victim of its own built-in paradox. On the one hand, because the appointments are short and because privacy for the interviews is limited, it could be argued that they are of little use, especially in a school that effectively manages its home–school contacts so that liaison continues throughout the year. On the other hand, however, the very existence of a parents' evening is clearly perceived as an important part of the same programme of home–school liaison. Certainly any attempt to abandon the practice would, in most schools, lead to a good deal of opposition and misunderstanding.

For most teachers, though, the biggest problem surrounding parents' evening is the often-observed tendency usually described as 'The parents you want to see never come'. This often remains true even when general attendance rates are encouragingly high. After all, in a class of thirty children there may only be two or three who are giving considerably more than the average amount of concern, but it is a fair bet that these are the ones whose parents will not come on parents' evening.

So how does the concerned teacher get the parents of 'problem' children to attend? The best way into an answer is to consider why they stay away. The reasons are varied, but may well be any mixture of the following.

Pupil Intervention

A child may manipulate things so that his or her parents stay away. At the most obvious level he will do this by failing to deliver the letter that contains the information. Slightly subtler ploys such as going home and declaring that all the appointments are 'booked up', or that the only appointments left are those that coincide with his or her mother's working hours. Many parents seem willing to accept verbal messages of this kind despite any amount of exhortation by the school to believe only official letters.

Unwillingness to be Exposed

Parents who know that their child is a 'problem' – either falling behing with work or constantly in trouble for misbehaviour – may be reluctant to attend a parents' evening and mix with smiling neighbours whose children are, apparently, models of endeavour and good conduct.

Sheer Lack of Interest

Teachers often assume that this is the main reason for not attending. It is, however, quite rare. Parents are, on the whole, genuinely interested in the education of their children. 'Apathy' – a word much used in staffrooms in this context – usually, on examination, turns out to mask something else.

Getting the unwilling ones in

The school may have a system for following up parents who do not turn up to parents' evening. If there is no system, a teacher could well suggest either that something general be done, or that he or she be allowed to follow up his or her own parents. The first step is a simple letter – 'Sorry you were unable to come to parents' evening. I would still like to see you. Please write on the bottom of this letter when you are able to get here. Give me more than one choice of time and date, and I will do my best to meet you on one of them'.

A further refinement is to ask the education social worker, or whoever performs this function, via the head, to deliver the letter or to deliver a verbal message and try to fix an appointment.

Occasionally, the parents of one child may retreat entirely from contact with the school, either refusing to acknowledge letters or, perhaps, making appointments and failing to keep them. The most usual reason for this is that the parents have decided that the school is simply saying the same thing over and over again; that they either do not agree with it or that they do agree to accept the recommendations that always follow – about statementing, perhaps. In the ideal world, of course, relationships would not be allowed to slide this far. In reality, however, they occasionally do.

This is enormously difficult to cope with. Most schools profess with a greater or lesser degree of emphasis that they depend upon home–school co-operation. Against this background, the withdrawal of one home from the contract becomes an immediate and severe problem.

The danger is that an escalating series of demands will be made, culminating in the carrying out of a threat to exclude the child from school unless the parents come in. Some schools have found a way round this kind of impasse by using the school governors. A pair of governors – it ought to be two – are briefed about the problem and visit the home. Their job is to listen and report back to the head – ultimately to the governing body. With their help, both the school and parents may be given the opportunity to make diplomatic and face-saving concessions that will, at least, get everyone talking to each other again.

Action checklist

1. Prepare carefully for parents' evening – room, notes, children's work.
2. Open the interview confidently and pleasantly.
3. Check the identity of child and of visitors.
4. Keep control of the timetable by referring parents on to the head or by making arrangements for a further interview on another day.
5. Keep the interview professional. Do not gossip.
6. Spend much of the time listening.
7. Do not write off or criticize parents who do not come – instead, devise a strategy for getting them in.

Part IV: The Curriculum

The word 'curriculum' is variously defined. It can, for example, simply mean the various core and foundation subjects of the National Curriculum. Or it can be taken to include all of the learning experiences, intended or unintended, the child experiences in school. Most usually, when teachers use the word curriculum, they mean something in between these two extremes – something broader than the legislative minimum, but also rather less than all-embracing. 'The intended learning experiences a pupil encounters in school', is perhaps as good an account as any.

Almost any curriculum area can bring problems to a child. Some, though, seem to throw up more than their fair share. Some of these are discussed in this part.

9
MATHEMATICS

Joanna Lumley was interviewing Sir Harry Secombe on the TV. 'I was no good at maths,' said Sir Harry, giving vent to that infectious chuckle.

'Nor I,' replied Joanna, while a million middle-aged men doted on her every word, 'It all passed me by completely'. Another comfortable chuckle and they passed on to something else.

What is it about maths? To be unable to read or write is considered a social disadvantage – indeed, there are those who consider that the notion of dyslexia was invented because middle-class families were unable to accept the simple notion of illiteracy. Nobody ever says, 'You'll have to read the programme to me, Darling, I'm hopeless at reading!' To be incompetent at number, however, is almost something to brag about. 'Oh, I'm no good at figures! I was terrible at maths when I was at school!'

It is interesting to speculate on the reasons for this. Reading is, of course, a very social activity – it is difficult to get through life as an incompetent reader, and in the past the ability to read was one of the things that distinguished the educated classes from the rest. While much the same can be said about number, it is probably true to say that skill with figures – and particularly the mental wizardry that used to be displayed, in the pre-electronic age, by bank clerks and shopkeepers – always had the taint of trade upon it. To be good at adding up meant, perhaps, that you were a wage slave. People of status did not need to add up – they just went into banks where clerks did it for them. Consequently it became acceptable – desirable even – to affect disdain for figures.

Once upon a time this attitude was reinforced by the school system. The elementary schools of a century ago had arithmetic on the curriculum. The public schools did not. Elementary schools prepared working-class boys and girls for trade and industry. Public schools prepared upper-class boys for leadership.

Neither was there much attempt to make arithmetic interesting. Learning to read, although it could be drudgery, always had the potential for escape in that you had to read *something* and there was always a chance that what you were reading would be interesting – perhaps even inspiring. The ability to write, too, could be liberating even though the process of learning to do it might be painful. Arithmetic, however, was always just figures. A very few children found that they were good at it, and derived pleasure from the ownership of a rare gift and from the sheer ability to do tricks with figures. Most youngsters, though, went through agonies of trying to learn processes that hard won, were quickly forgotten if not constantly practised.

The end result of all this is that when it comes to keeping children excited and interested, maths starts from behind, carrying kinds of social and historical handicaps. Children, of course, are not born with an aversion to maths; nor is there any sort of inherited folk memory. There are lots of environmental influences, however, that can help to persuade them that maths is unpleasant – their parents and relatives, for example, may tackle maths-related tasks with groans and forecasts of failure. 'You work this out, I can't!' Society as a whole is heavily skewed against the enjoyment of mathematics, so much so that the child who actually does get a kick out of it is often regarded as something of an oddity – a sort of mad professor figure.

Up to a point this is all quite light-hearted and relatively harmless. Unfortunately, however, there are some children whose aversion to number work is so strong that they become unhappy and reluctant to come to school, feigning illness or perhaps even playing truant.

It is important to realize that this particular problem may not be all that obvious. At any given moment there may be several children struggling with a particular maths topic, and the ones who are really unhappy, as opposed to the ones who are just fed up during the lessons, are not always easy to identify. The most unhappy child, in other words, may not be the one who is having the most apparent trouble with the subject.

Children will show their anxiety in various ways. One may find endless excuses for not tackling the new work – he or she may spend time covering his or her book, perhaps, or copying up work he or she missed earlier, or making a neater version of something done yesterday. Children are remarkably adept at making this kind of evasion while at the same time avoiding direct confrontation with the teacher. It is, incidentally, an entirely natural way of behaving. Avoiding unpleasant work is something all people, including teachers, will do unless they apply a little self-discipline or are leaned on by someone else. Another child may show his or her worry more directly, by coming constantly to the teacher for help. Now teachers expect children to come to them for help, but when the same child comes constantly, showing what seems to be a lack of initiative or a lack of desire to plunge in and have a go, the temptation is to end up by sending the questioner away with a sharp word – a happening that will often be resurrected by a worried parent at some later stage.

Excessive worry is also sometimes reported by a parent. There may be a phone call to the head or a note saying how bothered a child is by the new maths topic. It is a sign of the nature of the problem that such calls mentioning maths are relatively common, whereas calls that mention other classroom subjects are extremely rare. 'He's worried about Drama', for example, while being just about conceivable, sounds unusual enough to underline the point I am making.

How to tackle it? The basic thing is to make the subject just as interesting and exciting as any other. This, to say the least, is a tall order, and will not be entirely within the control of the class teacher anyway. There are, though, some basic ground rules. One is to manage children's mathematical learning in such a way that they are not presented with big learning steps in quick succession. Maths is best learnt in small steps with lots of reinforcement in between. It is the drive for fast progress that drops children by the wayside and causes them to have sleepless nights; and the drive for fast progress is itself caused by pressure from the teacher. This notion of 'pressure' is well within the control of the individual teacher, and deserves some consideration.

Maths is commonly perceived as a 'progressive' subject – which is to say that it is put together in such a way that pupils proceed up a ladder of skills, learning one and then going on to the next. Convention has it that this structure is stronger in maths than it is in other subjects – that you do not, for example, learn geography or English or history in quite the same way. Whether or not this notion holds good when you examine it closely is another matter. Suffice it to say that the subject is strongly perceived in this way. Thus in arithmetic, for example, you start by understanding the nature of simple numbers, then you learn to add them up and take them away; then you go on to multiply and divide. The processes get more complicated; the numbers get bigger. This description begs all sorts of questions; the point is not that it is necessarily accurate but that the subject, in school, has traditionally been perceived very much like this. What this means is that there is always competition and pressure to go faster up the ladder. A clever child is one who can do long multiplication at the age of 7. A slow child is one who is still adding single digits at the age of 9. One result of this is that children are very commonly moved on far too quickly, without the opportunity to consolidate each stage.

For example, it is generally accepted that children need lots of concrete experience in their early learning of maths – they need to use apparatus, to measure things, to pour water from one container to another – all the things that teachers are entirely familiar with. The problem is that because of the strength of the 'ladder' model in everyone's mind, this kind of activity is thought of as 'infant', 'elementary', 'easy' – the words always being used in a negative way. Many teachers will reject this sort of prejudice, but it remains true that some of their colleagues, and certainly many parents, will continue to believe that the main aim is to get children off apparatus and on to paper recording as quickly as possible.

So strong is this feeling that when I was head of a middle school, taking children at 8 from the first school, the head of the first school was moved to come and see me one day to explain carefully their new maths policy. It involved all of their children, up to the age of 8, doing far more practical, apparatus-based work than they had done before. What motivated her to visit me was to point out that she would be sending children on to us who may not, ostensibly, be as far on with their work as the intakes of previous years had been, but who ought to be much more confident about the basic processes. That she felt the need to explain this so carefully, feeling perhaps that we would be disappointed to be taking children who were not experienced in paper recording, demonstrates the point I am making.

In fact, of course, most children, right up to school-leaving age and beyond, could benefit from more practical work in mathematics – measuring, counting and using apparatus for shape and number. Children need strong reinforcement and practice at every stage, with frequent revision of what went before.

Most educators think that even very able children ought not to be raced on from stage to stage. 'Sideways enrichment' is the phrase often used – the child who has grasped a concept quickly, ahead of others in the class, should be given a wide variety of imaginative work that extends the same concept into other areas – applying it, using it imaginatively in a variety of contexts.

This, then, is the first recipe for avoiding some of the traditional maths traumas – to provide lots of work, plenty of learning experiences, but never to feel rushed into pushing any pupil on to the next stage before he or she is ready. And, in general, to be very generous in estimating the amount of time needed at each stage before moving on to the next. To a great extent this is a matter of resources. One problem about relying heavily upon a published maths scheme is that sheer lack of space prevents the inclusion of sufficient practice material at each stage. Often, to be fair; the teachers' handbook makes this absolutely clear – sometimes there is heavily emphasized, urgent advice to the teacher about supplementing the practice material. Occasionally it is possible to buy extension material that provides more practice. The trouble is though, that teachers too often skimp on their reading of the teachers' handbook and rely solely upon the pupil material for guidance, with the result that children simply do insufficient practice before moving on. The well-established, much-used and excellent Fletcher maths scheme, for example, has a thick and highly detailed teachers' handbook, and the scheme's authors make clear that this handbook is, in fact, the core of their work. Even so, it is possible to find inexperienced teachers using the scheme without proper and regular access to the handbook simply because the school does not have enough of them, or because no one has told the young teacher what to do. As a result there are classes being moved page by page through their Fletcher books in a way the authors never intended – a state of affairs almost guaranteed to produce anxieties in some of the children in any class. Supplementary advice, therefore, is to make sure that the published scheme is thoroughly understood; that the teachers' book is carefully studied and that extra material, where it is called for, is prepared. All this may require a lot of hard work and perhaps a lot of strength of mind, but in the end it is the right thing to do.

Ensuring that each child in the class is working at the right level – which is not easy, but ought to be the aim – ought to reduce to a minimum the amount of undue anxiety among them. The next step is to make sure that the classroom atmosphere in the maths lesson is as stress-free as possible. Some teachers, especially if they have had a bad time with maths themselves, give out anxiety signals to the class when maths lessons come around. They may even openly express disappointment that, say, art has to finish and maths take its place. 'Sorry, class, we've got to put this away. We may not like it but we've got to do some maths today.'

A lot of primary teachers hated maths themselves. A significant number had to struggle to get the basic GCE or GCSE maths pass necessary for qualified teacher status. It is never going to be easy for some of these teachers to avoid giving negative signals, however subtle, to their classes about the subject. A facial expression, a tone of voice, an almost subliminal show of reluctance to start the lesson will, over a period of weeks and months, build up into something that was certainly never intended but that will nevertheless be a very powerful influence. And because so many primary teachers are women, the danger is that the already apparent sex differences in attitudes to maths will be perpetuated. Put simply, it seems that in mixed learning groups boys tend to do better at maths than do girls. No woman teacher would want to reinforce this consciously. The danger lies not in what she says but in revealing her personal fears of the subject, and in unconscious signalling an expectation that boys are mathematicians and girls are not.

It follows that the primary teacher who brings to the school a bad experience of maths carries a very heavy responsibility not to pass this on to his or her charges. To begin with, perhaps, he or she should, while at college or university, have tried hard to do whatever maths education courses were available. Teaching students generally have a number of optional professional courses from which to choose. On the whole they either choose the things they like and are good at, or deliberately choose weak areas with a view to self-improvement. It hardly seems necessary to recommend the latter course – if it seems a sacrificial thing to do, it is worth remembering that endless generations of students have discovered new interests and new enthusiasms in this way.

If a student teacher's school maths experience was very traditional, then it becomes particularly important for something to be done about it, for the battle to improve the image of maths in the primary classroom is based upon teaching it in ways that are more relevant and exciting. A very large number of students find that, in their study of primary maths teaching, they themselves learn more mathematics than they have done in all of their schooling up to that point, and that concepts that have been life-long mysteries are suddenly unlocked and revealed in beautiful clarity. The new teacher who has missed all of this at college and who comes to the primary classroom still burdened with memories of algebraic misery needs, as a matter of urgency, to get on some in-service courses.

In the meantime, the important thing for the teacher to remember is that he or she owes it to his or her classes, in no uncertain way, to be positive and cheerful about maths lessons. They have to be tackled with an attitude free from any show of reluctance, however joky. If this is not done, there is a terrible danger that the timetable slot called 'maths' will start to separate itself out into a 'different' and less pleasant kind of experience; a time of tears and confrontation; a sort of unpleasant lump in an otherwise purposeful day.

This is not a book about the teaching of maths, and it is not possible to deal with all the possible difficulties that will bring children to a halt. It is, however, worth looking at what is probably the biggest block to under-standing and, therefore, the most common root cause of sleepless nights and tantrums. This is undoubtedly the concept of place value.

Our number system only works because of place value – the notion that a number has different meanings according to where it is 'placed'. Thus the digit '2', can mean 'two' 'twenty', 'two hundred', and so on, literally *ad infinitum*, depending upon where it is placed, this placing being defined by the filling in of empty spaces 'behind' the digit with zeros. It is not, to say the least, an easy concept to describe – my own description here is proof of that – and yet full and total familiarity with it is absolutely essential to all manner of arithmetical operations. There is no doubt that a very high proportion of primary-school children have still not understood the concept of place value when they leave for the secondary school. They may be able to parrot through some of the operations that ostensibly assume understanding, but in the end the conceptual gap will be exposed, and somewhere at some time, an unfortunate teacher is either going to have to go back to first principles or scrub round the missing knowledge as best he or she can. Needless to say, the latter course is the one most often adopted, so that as well as 11-year-olds who do not understand place value, we have 16-year-olds and, by implica-tion, adults whose arithmetical understanding is similarly fatally flawed.

There are, of course, all manner of techniques and methods for teaching and reinforcing the concept of place value, many of them using practical apparatus. The important thing for the teacher is to realize the amount of time it takes for some children to absorb the principle, and to be extremely patient and unhurried in helping children to get there. There is no rush – if there is, it should be resisted.

In the end, though, when the teacher has established a friendly, purposeful classroom where maths is fun, and where jolly displays about number and measurement line the walls, what does he or she do when there is still one child whose unhappiness and failure in maths is causing a major problem? For one thing, before that point is reached, there ought to be some help from the school's special-needs teacher. In many schools the special-needs provision concerns itself either exclusively or mainly with literacy – unsurprisingly, given the importance of this area and the scarcity of the resources with which schools have to work. The problem with this policy is that teachers can be left alone to struggle with children who are having numeracy problems. A teacher who feels beset in this way ought to be prepared to make his or her case in staff-meeting discussion.

Whatever the provision in school, most local authorities have some kind of support service for mathematics. There will be an adviser or inspector and, in addition, there may well be a team of advisory teachers, and perhaps a maths centre that will be a central point for advice and resources. On the whole, this kind of authority service will not want to intervene with a particular child. They may, however, respond to a general plea by an inexperienced teacher, channelled through the headteacher. And, of course, there are other support services – school psychologist, for example – for really difficult and unhappy cases.

So far as tackling the problem in class goes, however, the first point of contact, as always, is with the parent. Whether the parent has brought the problem up, or whether it has been observed by the teacher, there ought to be a meeting for an exchange of views. It may be, for example, that anxiety about maths is being generated in the home, perhaps as a result of parental pressure or of the transferance of parental feelings of inadequacy with the subject. All the things already discussed about subliminal anti-maths messages apply in the home as they do in school, and parents may well need to have this pointed out to them. As with reading, where anxiety on the part of parents turns, in the child, into fear and reluctance to try, so it is with maths, except that the messages are likely to be more subtle and difficult both to detect and to eliminate.

One issue that commonly arises in such discussions is that of homework. Anxious parents may well feel that if their child is falling behind, then he or she will catch up more quickly if he or she does some work at home. In all subjects this needs careful handling – see the general discussion on homework in Chapter 12 – but with maths the issue is even more delicate because, although practice at home can certainly help, it needs to be relaxed, unpressured practice. If parents can be persuaded of this, then giving homework is probably acceptable.

One parental attitude to maths that is quite common is that which says, 'It's all different from when I was at school. The maths is like a different subject'.

It is, of course, clear what this means. There probably was a time when, for most children at school, maths – at least in the primary and early secondary years – consisted largely of 'sums' and 'problems'. The basic arithmetical operations of adding, subtracting, multiplying and dividing, supported by rote learning of tables, took up most of the maths lesson. Things had already started to change in the late 1950s, however, and a very large proportion of the parents of primary-school children ought to be very familiar these days with such things as the use of structural apparatus and with colourful-looking maths-scheme books. The important thing is to reassure parents that although there is, and has been for some time, a continuous effort to make mathematics seem more attractive, and to introduce into the maths curriculum some principles that at one time were reserved for much later study, the basic aims are still the same. Few schools, for example, decry the rote learning of tables. It is, after all, extremely useful to know tables up to twelve and, although much is made of the notion that it is better to know how to work them out than to have them half-learnt, it is no great demand to expect an 11-year-old to be able to respond instantly when asked any multiplication up to twelve times twelve. The important thing, as with any other task involving the memory, is not so much the learning as the continuous practice, and a teacher who is determined that his or her class shall know, and remember their tables, can usually achieve it by dint of ten minutes a day application to the task. The children will, by the way, take great pride in their skill.

Action checklist

1. Do you have negative feelings about maths yourself? If so, there is a fair chance you will pass some of them on to the children.
2. To raise your own acceptance of the subject, get on some local-authority courses; ask for help from advisory teachers.
3. Never, ever, use maths as a punishment or expression of disapproval. 'Right, you're not doing games; you can do maths instead!'
4. Take *time* to see that concepts are established. Never feel rushed to get through the syllabus. A little understanding is better than a lot of confusion.
5. If there is a published maths scheme, *read the teachers' handbook*!
6. Think constantly of practical applications for maths – give children money to count; let them measure the hall for the school play. Use school and home problems to give practical problem-solving experience.

10
READING

Of all the learning experiences human beings have to undergo, that of acquiring the skill of reading is probably the most potentially traumatic. That we do not, as adults, usually perceive it like this is simply because it happened so long ago that we have forgotten what it was like. Much more recent learning experiences, such as having driving lessons, are fresh in our minds, and we dine out on our driving stories for years. That learning to drive is infinitely easier than learning to read – they are not in the same league at all – never occurs to us.

What complicates any discussion of learning to read is that, although we know it to be a hard-won and tremendously sophisticated affair, nobody is really sure exactly how the trick is accomplished. And in the absence of certainty about how reading is learnt, there is certainly no confident knowledge about how it can be taught. Some experts, indeed, are extremely dubious about the role of the teacher in the acquisition of reading, feeling that active teaching is at best ineffective and at worst actually harmful. This is probably the kind of over-statement people make in order to focus attention on a truth that lies a little further down the scale of radicalism. However, the fact remains that so long as there are so few certainties about how reading is learnt, it automatically follows that the role of the teacher is not something to be too certain of.

In illustration of this, it is necessary only to look at the long-running debate between those who want to teach reading by 'phonics' and those who believe in 'whole-word' methods. Give or take some differences of detail, this is a distinction between those who want children to learn to build up words from sounds denoted by letters – 'CAT' (each letter spoken phonetically) spells 'cat' – and those who believe that a child takes in the whole 'shape' of a word. Reading schemes may plump for one method or another and, although some schemes (and many teachers) hedge their bets by assuming that the truth lies in a compromise, there is still plenty of room for argument about the weighting to be given to each approach. The 'phonic' lobby, particularly, feels that just about every literacy problem up to, and including, dyslexia, is caused by ignoring phonics and teaching whole-word acquisition. The theory is that in learning the 'shape' of words, children bypass the structure and come out of the learning progress programmed with all kinds of misconceptions. After all, it is said, if you just learn words by their shapes you are not on the whole going to see much difference between 'dog' and 'bog', or between 'lion' and 'loin' – both these examples being very typical of the mistakes made by children who are having literacy problems at junior school. A child who had learned sounds, the argument goes on, would never make these mistakes, because whatever the similarities of appearance, these pairs of words make very different sounds.

Through this jungle the teacher has to carve a path. It is likely, however, that a school will have a policy, to which colleagues have to subscribe. Nevertheless, it is important that new teachers realize, first, that there is a tendency on the part of some colleagues to plug one reading method to the exclusion of all others and, second, that many of these same colleagues demonstrate a great deal more confidence about the teaching of reading than is probably justified by the state of our knowledge. At the end of the day, after all, although many children learn to read beautifully and speedily, and are entirely confident by the age of 8, a significant number are still having problems at the end of the junior school, and a proportion of them are still going to be in trouble when they leave school. If the confidence exuded by some reading experts was well-founded, reading failure would, presumably, never happen at all.

Dyslexia

Another argument about which new teachers need to be aware surrounds the subject of dyslexia. There have always been some children who, although apparently alert and able in all other aspects of school work, find the greatest difficulty in writing and spelling, so much so that their written work looks to the casual eye like gibberish. Letter reversals and transpositions of the kind described earlier are very characteristic of dyslexia, and in some children the problem seems to consist merely of a baffling and almost perverse tendency to regard 'b' and 'd' as interchangeable, despite the best efforts of teachers and parents to drum in what seems to them to be a pretty simple bit of knowledge. In other children this lack of awareness of letters and words is so serious that writing is entirely unrecognizable.

This specific difficulty – and it is regarded as 'specific' because it often does not seem to be a component of a more general learning problem – has commonly been described as 'dyslexia', and ascribed to a very localized malfunction of the brain. It is as if something, somewhere, inside the head is not making the right connections.

Talk to some teachers about this, however, and there will be a burst of apoplexy. Some – perhaps many – teachers and reading advisers simply find it impossible to accept the term 'dyslexia'. It is very important for teachers – especially inexperienced ones – to realize this, because dyslexia gets lots of publicity. There are some famous dyslexics; there are active and vocal dyslexia organizations; and the subject has been aired in television drama. Therefore, nothing is more certain than that at some time a teacher is going to be confronted by a parent who says that his or her child obviously 'has' dyslexia, and what is the school going to do about it?

Why are so many teachers and other educators so negative about dyslexia? The reasons are complicated. There is, for example, undoubtedly a feeling that dyslexia is a class issue – 'working-class children can't read and write; middle-class children have dyslexia', said one adviser I used to work with. It was his firm belief that dyslexia was a social concept invented to enable middle-class families to come to terms with the otherwise unacceptable fact that their child was having difficulty learning to read. 'My child is dyslexic', or, better still, 'My child has dyslexia', sounds better around the dinner table than 'My child can't read and write'. Such quasi-medical 'labelling' is a phenomenon well known to sociologists. There is also the fact that strong lobbying by those who believe in dyslexia has resulted in various concessions being made – to dyslexic children taking exams, for instance. Whether or not it is, in the last analysis, fair for 'dyslexic' children to be helped in this way when children with other sorts of learning difficulty are not is something that bothers many teachers.

There is also, perhaps, some room for discussion about whether the term 'dyslexia' actually helps. Believers clearly feel that it is helpful to categorize children in this way, because it provides a focus for study and for lobbying for provision. Another point of view is that to lump together a set of problems under a fancy name is to risk the label being a substitute for action.

Because this book is intended for young teachers, who are forming their own philosophies, it is important that I make my own stance clear. It has to be said that I am cautious about the label 'dyslexia'. It seems to me akin to calling a tummy-ache 'abdominagony' – the label sounds impressive and gives the sufferer something to brag about. In the end, though, the label itself is of no help, and can be a hindrance, in so far as it lumps together all kinds of problems and all kinds of children, all of whom have to be individually helped. Teachers and advisers have been helping children with learning difficulties for years. Neither the problems nor the techniques for dealing with them change just because the label changes.

Having said that, I have to point out that the 'dyslexia lobby' is powerful and vociferous, and has some very big guns firing on its behalf. The new teacher who wants to find out about dyslexia has lots of sources to refer to. What is important is for him or her to remember that this is a subject on which passions run very high. Parents who feel that dyslexia accounts for their own child's literacy problems may become impatient with the school, while headteachers and reading advisers may turn out to be less than enthusiastic about the whole business. The class teacher can very easily be in a difficult position in all of this. He or she might be sympathetic with the parents – perhaps impressed by what they have to say, especially if they have taken advice from an independent source of information on dyslexia – and yet constrained by a school or local-authority policy that takes a different line.

The important thing to bear in mind is the welfare of the child. What is unforgiveable is for a child to become the victim of strained relations between school and parent. The class teacher has a key role to play here, and one that demands a great deal of tact. The teacher must not, for example, seem to be saying to parents, 'I agree with you, but my hands are tied'. Simple loyalty and professionalism precludes it. The acceptable formula is for the teacher to say that he or she cannot take sides, but that he or she can give advice on how to proceed and whom to see in pursuing the argument further. By writing down the address of the area education office, and the name of the officer who has the job of listening to parental queries, a teacher can retain the friendship and trust of a parent while at the same time keeping loyal to his or her school.

Stress

Learning to read can be a very stressful business. What many adults do not always realize, though, is that a great deal of the stress on the child comes from outside. Think, for example, of what happens in the typical primary classroom. The teacher is 'hearing readers'. This means, often, that the teacher sits at the desk, with the reading record file open, and calls children to him or her one at a time to stand by him or her and read from their current reading book. For the good reader this is often a valued and enjoyable time. A good reader will often eagerly volunteer to read, and be disappointed if the lesson goes by with no opportunity to take a turn. Think a little further, however, and consider what the same experience brings to the child who is having reading difficulty. He goes out to the front and begins to make halting progress down the page. He is all the time aware of the silent class, and is convinced that they are all listening to his mistakes. Out of the corner of his eye he can see Samantha and Robert, who are skilful readers. He is convinced that they are staring at him, or glancing meaningfully at each other. From time to time a word brings him to a complete halt. The teacher waits – perhaps tapping a pencil or simply breathing – the tension mounts and the word becomes less rather than more intelligible the more it is stared at. The teacher gives a little help – pointing to a part of the word, perhaps, or uttering the first sound. The fact that this bit of assistance is of no help at all just makes the whole fraught business into even more of a nightmare.

Much the same can happen at home. A parent is probably aware that his or her son needs practice in reading, so he or she asks the child to read. The parent, however, is very tense when he or she hears the child read because he or she is aware of potential failure, and fearful of what it means in the long run. Frustration and emotion occasionally combine to make the parent angry, and he or she calls the son names he or she instantly regrets. The child hurls down the book and runs weeping from the room.

As if all of that were not enough, the child who is failing at reading is surrounded by reminders of the difficulty. Children who read well – many of them much younger than this child is – stand up in assembly and perform impeccably with scripts, bibles and books of various kinds. Perhaps the child has a younger brother or sister who reads better – and perhaps, sadly, adults in the family are tactless about drawing attention to this.

It ought not, therefore, to be all that surprising when a child with a reading problem develops behaviour problems as well. To begin with, the child may simply show reluctance to be put into a position where the failure is apparent. The child will 'forget' to take his or her reading book home, and in class will gaze about and seem 'unable to concentrate'. In passing, let me say that 'inability to concentrate' is surely a red herring. All human beings, of whatever age and ability level, are able to concentrate on things that attract them. Many a slow learner with a 'limited attention span' can be found spending hours playing pool, or fishing, or mending bikes. Similarly, a teacher who finds if difficult to give an hour's undivided attention to the marking of a set of books may have no problem at all in playing chess for three hours. In the context of classroom learning, 'inability to concentrate' really means 'unwillingness to engage the task'. This is important, because 'inability' implies that the teacher cannot really do anything about it, whereas 'unwillingness' is firmly in the teacher's domain.

What is surprising is not that children with reading problems have other kinds of problems too, but that so many of them do not. Every primary school will have some children whose worrying behaviour is at least connected with a learning difficulty. Equally, though, every primary school will have lots of children who are eagerly and cheerfully trying hard to improve their reading. The child with furrowed brow, finger on the page, fighting his or her way down the page of a reading book, always ready to look up and smile at a visitor and respond to a word of praise or encouragement is a very common sight. It is no exaggeration to say that the tenacity and optimism of so many children provide an example for all of us.

Advising parents

When a child is having reading problems, parents will inevitably be involved. In this day and age there is no school that wants to shut parents out of the learning process, but even if there were, parents are generally so aware of the importance of learning to read that if there is an obvious problem they will surely become involved – either by putting on pressure at home or by visiting the school. The days when teachers could say, 'We are the experts, forget it and leave it to us', are gone – if they were ever here. Sooner or later, therefore, either at a parents' evening or at a specially arranged interview, a teacher is going to be face to face with a parent who is worried about the reading progress of his or her child.

There are three important things for the teacher to get across in any such meeting. The first is to convince the parent that the school takes the matter seriously. The second is to persuade the parent not to show too much anxiety in front of the child. The third, and perhaps most important, is to tell the parent that he or she can actually provide important positive help.

The first of these is necessary because a parent is anxious and thus likely to think that the school is making light of the problem. This feeling may be compounded when the staff of the school, trying hard to not to provoke the parent into too much anxiety, adopts a cheery, positive approach – 'Don't worry about it, Mrs Smith. He'll come along in time I'm sure!' The way round this is to present facts. Telling the parent, in a professional and businesslike way, what the exact position is – reading progress as compared with the expected progress for a child of that age, illustrated with information about what material the child is reading, and some detail about what exactly the specific problems are, will go some way to convincing the parent that the teacher is at least aware, in an organized way, of what the nature of the difficulty is. Similarly, hard information about what the school is providing – frequency of classroom reading practice, the way that this is organized, extra help from a specialist teacher – all of this is considerably better than just saying, 'We are doing the best we can'. There should be no professional secrets in this area.

It really is important that parents should be made aware of exactly what the nature of the difficulty is. The tendency in schools is for children to be praised and encouraged, to the extent that their parents think they are making better progress than they are. Thus, a phrase from a teacher like, 'He's done really well at his reading this term, Mrs Smith', can be extremely misleading. Teacher might simply mean that the child has worked gamely and cheerfully for twelve weeks. What he or she may not say is that his actual measured progress during that time has really been minimal – the omission arises partly from the teacher's instinct to be positive and to give praise wherever possible and partly from an inability to admit fully the lack of progress even to him or herself. Something inside of the teacher is saying, 'He works so hard, he must be getting somewhere'. Life, alas, is not always as fair as this. The parents, for their part, interpret the teacher's praise and optimism as meaning that their child is making great strides with his reading.

Such misunderstandings are extremely common. They usually lead to some kind of grief – perhaps when a child moves class or moves school, and another teacher spells out the true story. 'But he was doing so well with Mrs Johnson'. Needless to say, many a tale of professional ill-will between one teacher and another or between schools arises out of stories like this.

What teachers need to remember is that although encouragement, optimism and searching out the positive all constitute essential parts of the primary philosophy, it is necessary to be careful that this attitude does not extend to misleading parents into thinking that their children are making better progress than they actually are. What parents need, and are entitled to, are facts about the attainment of their child by comparison with the rest of the population as a whole, not just by comparison with the other children in the same class.

One way of providing information about reading progress, of course, is to use reading ages. One problem with this is that reading ages are derived in different ways, by different tests, not all of which are equally good. Another difficulty arises from the apparently precise nature of the reading age – 'Her reading age is 12.5' looks pretty exact, but disguises the fact that nobody, least of all the people who devised the test in the first place, would want to say that it is anything more than an approximation within defined limits. The misunderstanding is compounded by using the terms 'chronological age' and 'reading age' alongside each other, sometimes abbreviated on a record sheet to 'CA' and 'RA'. This implies that the two are in some way alike, whereas they are most certainly not. Chronological age is objectively fixed and measured in a way that reading age never can be, but by putting them together, the one seems to give extra validity to the other.

If a school tests for reading age, and keeps records, then parents need to know what the records say for their respective children. The teacher, therefore, has a considerable responsibility when it comes to telling parents exactly what the reading age means. In particular, it really is important to point out that small changes in reading age mean very little.

Not all schools give formal tests for reading age. The reason, quite simply, is that a formal test gives no better information than a teacher can provide from observing a child's performance with regard to the material provided for reading. If the school uses a graded reading scheme, and the teacher is using it properly, with due regard to the handbook and other support material, then any given child's reading performance by comparison with the age-group will be a matter of record. The fact that this may not be expressed with the decimal point precision of a reading age is no bad thing, given that this apparent precision is in fact entirely spurious.

The first thing, then, when talking to parents about a child's reading progress is to make sure that they are given a good idea of the school's judgement about the child's performance, while at the same time being helped to understand that measuring reading performance is fraught with difficulty and that any numbers quoted do not have a high degree of objective accuracy.

The next thing is to talk to the parents about what they can do to help. Parents usually want to help but are often reluctant to do so because they see the teaching of reading as an expert business for which they are not qualified. This is often compounded by the fact that the parents of children with learning difficulty have often themselves experienced the same sort of problem and are left with a lack of confidence in their ability to provide worthwhile help. The most important thing, therefore, is to try to demystify the process, so that parents come to see that helping a child with reading is really a loving, accepting sort of activity – a part of family life – and is by no means a hard-nosed pedagogic exericse.

Here are some principles the teacher can introduce to parents who want to help children with reading.

Avoid Stress and Anxiety

The process must be stress and anxiety-free. This is the first and great commandment. Somehow, no matter how worried the parent is, reading in the home must be a quiet and relaxed activity. It is not easy to achieve this. The parents of a child with reading problems are usually very anxious. This may show itself in impatience with the child, in family rows which the child lies in bed listening to, and in all manner of verbal and non-verbal hints that parents are worried. At the most extreme, a parent will seize on a child as soon as he or she comes in from school, sit him or her down and make him or her read aloud. Impatience rising by the minute, the parent sits uttering sighs and muttered imprecations and ends up losing control and shouting. It is not, of course, always as bad as this, but there are lots of steps on the way to this, and children are very quick to pick up parental anxiety and to take the natural step of avoiding the situation that leads to it.

Patience

With patience and a little guile, a parent may inveigle a child into voluntarily turning out the reading book. In some families, indeed, the trust and confidence is already there to enable the child to enlist the help of a parent. Or the parent might casually pick up the reading book and say, 'This your reading book? Maybe we'll have a look at it after tea'.

Listening Abilities

The important thing for the parent to do is to listen. The reading time can be a very loving and valuable time – an opportunity, perhaps, for a father to spend more time than he otherwise might alone with a son or daughter. When the child stumbles over a word, or comes to a complete stop, then help should be given unhesitatingly, especially in the early days when the priority is to remove anxiety.

A Willingness to Help

Educational expertise is not needed. What is needed is time, attention and stress-free listening. It is not even all that necessary for the parent to be an excellent reader. There are lots of examples of parents who read English only with difficulty providing help for their children simply by being willing to listen and give stress-free time.

Content

What is read is less important than that reading should happen. If the child wants to read a comic to his or her parents, then so be it. It may be good for him or her to have an escape from the demands of the school reading scheme. It is worth remembering that every child – perhaps every adult too – will turn occasionally with relief to reading material that is 'too easy'. It is important not to turn this into a moral issue, for there is no law that says that everyone has to read to the limit of his or her ability all the time. Every athlete likes to go for a jog.

Contact

It is important for parents and teachers to keep in touch. Some schools have formal systems intended to integrate the efforts of home and school. Some reading schemes have material specifically intended to develop this link. It may not, however, always be necessary to build a highly developed system – and it may not be possible for the individual class teacher to start it on his or her own anyway. It is certainly possible, however, for parent and teacher to meet on a regular basis to compare notes, and for the essentials of these notes to be agreed and added to the child's reading record.

Professional Guidance

Although there has to be partnership between parent and teacher, the teacher should assume the professional role. The parents expect this – indeed they have the right to expect it. This does not mean, however, that teacher should be patronizing towards the parents, or should blind them with so much pseudo-science that they become discouraged. The most important thing is to help parents see that their own unique position has both advantages and disadvantages. The advantages are to do with being close to the child and aware of his or her needs. The disadvantages are largely to do with the effects of anxiety. As we have seen, anxiety itself is bad in that it transmits itself to the child. It impinges in other ways, too. It gives rise, for example, to the parent sometimes over-estimating the rate of the child's progress. When a teacher is guiding a child through the process of learning to read, he or she is careful to make sure that there is evidence of the child understanding what has been read – the teacher will ask some questions about it and have a conversation about the story. A parent, however, keen to see his or her child making progress and 'getting on to the next book', may well accept a gabbled, more-or-less correct reading that shows little real understanding. A child may bring a book back to school with a note saying, 'John has read the whole book to me in one evening. Please send another one'. This may sometimes be acceptable, but there will also be times when such an action will drive a coach and horses through the teacher's efforts to help the child read carefully and with understanding. The answer, as always, is for careful liaison between teacher and parent.

Pace of Learning

Teacher should explain to parents that reading progress does not necessarily proceed along a steady upward slope. Learning of any kind – to play an instrument, to drive, to do the Boston Two-step – is a matter of bursts of progress interrupted by frustrating plateaux and tear-provoking backward slides. Children, perhaps more than adults, are extremely erratic in their learning progress. One obvious problem is caused by the way that school holidays suddenly arrive just when there is, at last, some genuine forward movement. The long summer holiday would be interruption enough on its own, but there is always the added trauma of a change of class or even a change of school. Parents have to be prepared for the fact that the move from infant to junior school, taking place as it does across a six- or seven-week break, almost invariably involves some backsliding. This is most usually seen in the way that the new junior-school child is seen by his or her parents to be reading books that are easier than the ones he or she was on at the top of the infants school. It is not just that he or she has 'forgotten what he or she learnt'. There is also a factor connected with the child's need to find security and success in the new environment. Again, parents have to be reassured carefully about this, and told that the 'lost' ground – if that is what it is – will be made up in quick time provided that everyone keeps their heads and that there is no undue worry or pressure.

Loaning Materials

It should be possible for books to go home from school. Some schools have a very preservative attitude to their books, and hardly ever allow them out of the building. This may be understandable in the light of the financial battle all schools have to fight, but it is at least arguable that to work like this is to allow the financial tail to wag the educational dog. Many children – and it is a fact of life that this is particularly true of children with reading difficulties – live in homes where there is very little reading material. Such children must take books home. Whatever system the school or the teacher devises to keep track of books is a matter for them, but one way or another a way has to be found of allowing books to go home.

Action checklist

1. Read aloud to your class so frequently that colleagues comment on it.
2. Don't be dogmatic about methods of teaching reading – nobody has all the answers.
3. Take your time making up your mind about dyslexia – but remember that the label is not a substitute for action.
4. Remember, though, that the dyslexia lobby has gathered a lot of expertise about teaching reading.
5. With the school, work out a strategy for helping parents who come in armed with dyslexia information. Accept: don't feel threatened!
6. Make reading enjoyable and stress-free.
7. Help parents to help – be open, but stress the importance of being relaxed.
8. The child comes first. An anxious, stressed child will make little progress.

11
THE CHILD WHO DISLIKES PE, GAMES AND SWIMMING

Physical education, in various guises, takes up a surprisingly high proportion of the primary-school teaching week. Typically, there will be one forty-minute lesson a week of class PE and a whole afternoon of games – a total, perhaps, of two and a half hours out of a week of twenty-six hours. Additionally, many schools run a programme of visits to the local swimming baths – although swimming may not involve all of the children all of the time, and sometimes replaces either PE or games. Clearly the primary school's traditional commitment to physical activity is emphatic and unmistakable.

Equally emphatic is the determination, across primary and secondary stages, both to make all such physical activity compulsory for all pupils and to bolster it with various traditional rules about dress and attitudes. Thus a teacher may well find him or herself applying a school policy on PE clothing that looks something like this:

- *PE* To be done in white T-shirt, white gym shorts and gym shoes or bare feet.
- *Games* To be done in dark shorts and correct top and footwear for whatever sport is on the curriculum at the time. A tracksuit may be compulsory. A towel to be brought, and all children to have a shower.

- *Swimming* Plain bathing trunks or costume – no flowery outfits or loose shorts. Caps may be compulsory. Goggles optional. Pupil must provide his or her own towel, clearly marked with name and school. Often, money must be brought either for the bus or for admission to the pool.

This sort of full house rules is at the extreme end of a long spectrum, but it is an approach that is not at all uncommon, especially in affluent areas where there is general parental approval for dress rules. The problem is that these rules, devised by headteachers and approved of by governors, have to be enforced, in the first, instance by the class teacher.

Even in less rule-bound establishments, there are usually some basic requirements. Almost every school will demand some sort of clothing change for PE and games, and a school that has the facilities will commonly impose compulsory showers. Similarly, children will have no choice about whether or not to take part in PE or games or swimming. They are, it is reasoned, a legitimate and important part of the curriculum, and it follows that children should no more negotiate their participation in PE than they do their attendance at a maths or science lesson (it is, of course, possible to question the logic of this stance, but the fact remains that the argument is commonly used).

Some schools will excuse children from physical activity if they 'bring a note'. Even this concession, though, is often opposed by teachers who feel that a child who is fit enough to be at school is, by definition, fit enough to participate in the whole curriculum.

Problems

Enough has been said so far to demonstrate that the whole field of school physical activity is fraught with potential for conflict. How and why do these conflicts occur?

Lack of Organization

Getting to school with the right clothes on the right day is a demanding task for a young child. The routine may call for PE shorts and shoes on Tuesday; swimming costume and towel on Wednesday; hockey boots, shorts and showering towel on Friday. There are plenty of well-paid and well-organized adults who could be relied upon to get the sequence wrong at least one week in four. Then, of course, it all presupposes a high degree of parental support

– the right kit has to be clean and ironed for the right day. The more you look at it, the more it seems likely that in a school with a very strict 'kit' regime, the only children who are going to keep consistently out of trouble are those with boundless enthusiasm, backed up by a machine-like domestic routine. Anyone who flags, whose parents are even normally slapdash, or whose washing-machine is on its last legs, is headed for trouble.

Physical Self-Awareness

That feeling of depression generated by regarding one's own body is familiar enough to all but the most narcissistic of adults. Maturity, though, usually brings along the mental attitude to deal with it – we either avoid activities that expose our sags and blemishes or we have enough bottle to lollop around in brazen unconcern. Sometime during primary-school years, though, most children begin that agonized period of consciousness of the physical self that reaches a peak in early adolescence.

The problem for children is that changing for games involved undressing in front of others – often, in the primary schools, members of the other sex. Children who are over-weight may hate being exposed like this, as may children who are slow to develop sexual characteristics – hair, breasts – will be embarrassed if their friends are all ahead.

The most common cause of difficulty here is obesity. Fat children, whose self-consciousness is commonly reinforced by name-calling, are often agonizingly embarrassed about changing and showering. Even if they can some-how avoid attention in the changing-room, simply appearing in games kit and being made to attempt feats of athleticism will disturb many over-weight children.

Self-consciousness about Dress

I once taught a little girl whose knickers not only had legs in them but had been hand-knitted by her mother. Not surprisingly she was reluctant to change for PE. Holey socks, grimy underpants, long johns, lack of a vest can all become causes of distress, as can items that need dexterity to fasten and unfasten. By no means are such problems caused by parental inadequacy or neglect. Anxious parents who want children to 'wrap up warm' can unwittingly cause just as much heartache. And such is the strength of peer pressure and the hold clothing conventions have over even very young children that tantrums can be brought about by tiny deviations. Underpants with teddy bears on them may be anathema to a 11-year-old whose friendship group is aspiring to greater sophistication.

Physical Inabilities

The fundamental assumptions are still alive and well – that little girls skip and play two-ball against the wall, while little boys push and shove, play impromptu games of football and climb trees.

These stereotypes linger on in too many places. Even more persistent, though, is the equally powerful stereotype that sees the normal child as physically active and skilful. The expectation that a child can dodge and run, climb fearlessly, accurately throw and catch and generally be enthusiastic when asked to attempt a new physical task, is very strong.

In fact a significant minority of children are poor at catching and throwing, and will consequently seek to avoid having to do them. Similarly there are children – perhaps the same ones – who are mortally afraid of having to climb ropes or launch themselves over a vaulting horse. There are also children – again, perhaps the same ones, perhaps not – whose gait is observably ungainly, and will avoid having to run in public, for fear of looking foolish. The thought of being immersed in the swimming pool frightens some children, too.

Some of these perceived inadequacies have visible causes, of which obesity is, again, a common one. Often, though, there is no apparent reason for them, although there is a possibility that very minor birth damage to the brain may cause a child to be noticeably 'clumsy'.

Where do such fears and apparent inadequacies lead, and what can the primary-school class teacher do about them? Clearly, the most obvious way in which any of these self-doubts and perceived inadequacies show themselves is in the child's reluctance to do PE or games. If the school's policy is to run a fairly traditional and compulsory physical activity programme, the reluctant child will usually use one or both of two strategies. He or she will either 'forget' to bring his or her kit (or 'lose' it) or he or she will bring a note excusing him or her on medical grounds. In a school with firm kit rules, the child without kit is difficult to deal with. Making the child do it in his or her street clothes, for example, may result in their being dirtied or damaged. As a result, the child will often succeed in avoiding the activity, and this success will then reinforce his or her behaviour so that his or her arrival at school with no kit becomes a persistent and intractable problem for the teacher. Such children may end up being punished every week by detention and/or by being given unpopular and unpleasant work to do during the games period. It is worth reflecting on the strength of the internal pressures that will cause an otherwise co-operative pupil to risk disapproval and punishment over this issue. There are, surely, all sorts of implications for the school's ethos and philosophy.

The business of 'bringing a note' is altogether more complicated. At one extreme is the games enthusiast who breaks an arm falling from a tree at home, but who pesters his or her parents until he or she is allowed to come to school in plaster. The parents have to write or phone in unequivocal terms, lest the child attempts rope-climbing one-handed. At the other extreme is the child who seems always in perfect health but who regularly brings notes on games or swimming day asking to be excused on the grounds of a cold. Sometimes the note is precautionary and asks for the child to be excused, 'As she gets a cold when she walks home with wet hair'.

The usual staffroom reaction to this, not at all uncommon, pattern is to blame the parents for being over-protective. Be that as it may, it is worth considering that a child who likes physical activity will rarely allow her parents to excuse him or her for any except the most serious cause. Conversely, a parent who is not, at heart, supportive of a child's avoidance of games may write a note as the only workable alternative to a terrible scene or even flat refusal to go to school.

How does the class teacher deal with this?

To begin with, the teacher must run, in so far as it is possible within the school's curriculum policy, a physical activity programme that defuses problems before they occur. A good teacher does not, for instance, force an unwilling child to attempt, in front of the rest of the class, a rope climb or a vault. Physical education these days is much more concerned with personal development and with finding and building upon each individual child's strengths. Nevertheless, children are strongly driven by the cultural conventions of competitiveness and 'showing off', and given the slightest encouragement will climb, leap and spring in an orgy of competitive display that has the overt purpose of reinforcing the unofficial class pecking-order. An unperceptive teacher will too often allow this to go on, or may even reinforce it – 'Come on then, John, you show us how it's done!' What the teacher should be doing is encouraging and coaching each child to make some individual progress, however modest, and constantly presenting each small advance as a matter for rejoicing by the whole group.

The school's policy for games and PE will – or should – be clearly stated, and overseen by a teacher with responsibility for the subject and for the equipment. The policy may be 'traditional' encompassing coaching in the traditional team games, and gym exercises with and without apparatus. Or it may be more liberal, with games lessons that introduce children to a whole range of individual and paired, as well as team, activities, and gym work that centres around movement, dance and 'educational' gymnastics. To the extent that a school is committed to a basic approach, the freedom of the class teacher may be restricted.

The teacher's personal and pedagogic approach, however, is not, and his or her purpose, if conflict is to be avoided, is plain. The teacher must protect the unwilling or unskilled child from ridicule and macho down-putting. At the same time, he or she must work with the class to free them from traditional assumptions and help them to see the value of co-operation and of using their skills to help those less fortunately endowed. None of this is easy. It presupposes, for one thing, that the approach to physical activity must begin in the classroom, with the teacher attempting to forge a caring and co-operative attitude among the pupils.

Similarly, if the school makes demands about dress for physical activity, then the way the teacher presents these demands can either worsen class relationships or strengthen them. At the most basic level it is a matter of simple class organization to write on the blackboard at the end of the day, 'PE kit tomorrow', or to set up a system of interchangeable cardboard notices that will be looked after with religious zeal – and with greater reliability than most teachers could attain – by a couple of enthusiastic pupils.

Really forgetful children, however, need more help than this. The class, for example, can be organized so that the enthusiasts put reminder notes into the lunchboxes or schoolbags of the 'forgettors'. Or enthusiasts can be encouraged to call at a 'forgettor's' home in the morning, to issue an on-the-spot, last-minute reminder.

A slightly more drastic, but entirely practical, solution is for the teacher to keep a small emergency supply of kit – a towel, some shorts, perhaps a couple of pairs of gym shoes. There are various ways by which such a supply can be built up – often a word with the caretaker will produce items of long-unclaimed lost property. Perhaps the best strategy, though, is to enlist the support of the class, so that they see the solving of a classmate's problem as a co-operative venture. Many children will possess spare kit, which they will donate to a class 'kit box'.

Contact with parents

Whatever coping strategies are devised for keeping an unwilling pupil out of trouble, a child's continued unwillingness to do school physical activity is something that teacher and parent should discuss. Together, perhaps, they can work out a coping strategy.

To begin with, the class teacher should see if the parents can shed light on the reason for unwillingness – the child may have told his or her parents about being bullied or name-called in the changing-rooms, for example, and may have given in to his or her plea to write excuse notes. On the other hand, the teacher may be able to help parents by explaining the child's self-consciousness about underwear.

If obesity is at the root of the problem, the teacher may be able to explain just how distressed the child really is – the parents may under-estimate their child's anxiety. Despite a school of thought that believes the concept of being 'over-weight' to be largely social and fashion-dictated, there is a case for saying that obese children should be helped. They are commonly bullied or name-called, and all physical activity, including dance and drama, can become a cause of misery – and this is before any consideration of the health aspects. The parents of obese children should be urged to consult their doctor for referral to a dietician, and the class teacher should offer support to the child in following the diet, enlisting, again, the co-operation of the class.

Where a significant proportion – say a quarter – of a class is showing persistent unwillingness to do physical activity, interviews with parents may reveal a general feeling of discontent – about regular bullying in the changing-rooms, for instance, by a group of children, or about the school's dress regulations. Whatever these feelings are, they cannot, and should not, be ignored. In some cases the remedy is in the teacher's hands. If changing-rooms are properly run and supervised, for example, there should be no opportunity for bullying. Some teachers are remarkably trusting about this. What looks like a cheerful gang of boys, all chattering and trying to disentangle their vests, may actually be a minor hotbed of aggression and fear, the smiling faces being adopted like masks as soon as teacher opens the door. Continuous supervision of a changing-room is not easy – there is usually apparatus to be put away, shower taps to be turned on, other children to be looked after – but with a bit of care suspected bullies or their victims can be watched and brought out as soon as they are changed. The important thing is not to be too trusting, and not to leave the children unattended for too long.

Another general cause of dissatisfaction may be the school's policy towards games and PE kit. While some parents approve of elaboration in this area, there will be some who do not, and a group of less affluent familes may well be worried. Their feelings may be well hidden, emerging only gradually in parent interviews and through parent-governors. When they do, the issue becomes one for the head and the governors to decide, but every class teacher has access to both, and can also remind parents of their rights of access.

Another common cause of parental worry is where a teacher, either on his or her own initiative or as part of school policy, has a very 'Spartan' approach to games, and insists on taking children out in shorts on freezing cold days. A cross-country run in the snow, with a good watersplash will probably produce a small crop of protests.

Part of the problem here is that the teacher him or herself may hail from the kind of background and schooling where the goose-pimple approach to games lessons was part of the pattern of life. These colleagues are commonly nonplussed by the reaction of urban families for whom rain, snow and temperatures below freezing are things to be hurried through as fast as possible on the way home. What matters here is good sense. The children should be watched, and those genuinely distressed by cold should be sent in early. It is as well, too, if the teacher does not wrap up too warmly. The line, 'I understand you were wearing a warm track suit', appears in many of the complaints about cold-weather games! Provided that all the precautions are taken, and that the head is kept fully in the picture, it can help children to challenge them in this way, and there really are times when parents need to be told, however gently, that children can run through mud and water without catching pneumonia, and that they may actually enjoy the experience.

12
HOMEWORK

Regular homework is part of the pattern of life in most secondary schools. Part of the induction process of the new secondary-school entrant is to be given a homework diary and a homework timetable. The ritual of giving in homework, having it marked and the issuing of stern warnings and punishments to those who have not done their homework is a great part of secondary-school life. One of the problems about it is that teachers often find the giving and marking of homework to be a terrible bore. It often means scratching about at the end of a lesson – usually after the bell has gone, and time pressure is becoming intolerable – to find some sort of time-filling task to give. 'Read Chapter Five!' the teacher cries despairingly – and the conscientious children write this in their homework diaries, while others read his or her tone and the nature of the task to mean that they can simply do nothing at all. In some secondary schools the senior management team operate a homework checking system – calling in, for example, each day, the homework of a random sample of pupils. This is usually interpreted by junior members of staff as being more a means of keeping them on their toes than of checking the diligence of the pupils. The problem for senior management is that they usually make a big point of homework at parents' meetings and in the school brochure – 'Homework is regularly set. Each parent will have a copy of the homework timetable, and can assume that homework will be set in accordance with it. If a pupil regularly claims to have no homework, or to have done it in a very short time, parents are urged to query this with the year head . . .' And in its turn, all of *this* is dictated by a belief that parents want homework – like uniform, it makes the school appear serious and academically minded. It is generally assumed that parents admire the 'grammar school' image – white shirts, school ties, blazers, satchels, homework, speech day, teachers in suits, school teams – and very many secondary schools, in pursuit of a good local image and thus a sizeable intake of pupils, are willing to go along with it all.

The question here is to what extent primary schools do, or should, give homework for the same kind of reasons. There is no doubt that the same pressure for 'image' exists at primary level. Very many primary schools, for example, have uniform. Some have 'houses' and 'house points'. Homework, very often, is part of the same structure, and has relatively little to do with any educational discussion about whether it is a good idea or not.

Factors to consider

Fortunately for the teachers, however, it is extremely rare for the homework system to be as strong in the primary school as it can be in the secondary sector. Many primary schools give no formal homework at all. Some have a formal structure for the oldest age-group. Some leave it entirely to the discretion of the teacher. In deciding whether or not to give homework, there are a number of things to take into account.

Unfairness

Homework is intrinsically unfair in that some children have better facilities than others for doing it. One child may have his or her own room, a ready supply of stationery and reference books, and parents who will take an active and supportive interest in what he or she is doing. Another child, faced with the same task, may have to attempt it on a corner of the dining table with the television on in a corner, a crying baby in the other and an assortment of brothers and sisters trying hard to distract him or her. Should he or she have forgotten to take a ruler home, there may be none in the house to use.

All this seems obvious enough. The implication, though – which is often not properly thought through – is that if the teacher of these two children makes homework into an important and integral part of the curriculum, then he or she is at a stroke strongly reinforcing the inequalities that exist between them. This, needless, to say, is the exact opposite of what he or she ideally should be doing.

Purpose

What is the homework actually going to be for? It is probably not enough that it should simply promote the academic image of the school – therefore there has to be some sort of educational purpose in setting it. The most obvious answer to this is that the process of learning often involves lots of practice of learned operations. This is best illustrated by considering the process of learning a musical instrument. In formal music tuition, face-to-face contact with the teacher, although vital, is only effective if backed up by lots of private practice. The usual pattern is of a thirty-minute intensive lesson, then an hour or so a day of private practice for a week, then another intensive lesson at which the learned techniques are checked and some new ones introduced. Many instrumental teachers, especially of advanced students or of children over the age of about 7, cannot function at all if the pupil is not doing private practice.

It seems reasonable to extend this principle to the classroom – to say that a child can practise maths, or map work, or descriptive writing, at home, thus freeing pupil–teacher contact time for more productive teaching. This model envisages a classroom full of children with their heads down 'practising' while their teacher twiddles his or her thumbs or engages in fairly low-level checking of what is being done.

My own view is that this notion really does not stand up to scrutiny. To begin with, there is really no reason to suppose that the 'tuition-plus-practice' model is so desirable that it deserves imitation. On the contrary, it has grown up because it is the only sensible way for a music teacher with lots of individual pupils to work. A child, especially a very young one, would learn the piano or the violin or whatever much more quickly if he or she could have a daily ten-minute session or a series of short sessions spread through the day, and if he or she could learn as one of a class this could be an advantage rather than a handicap. Various tuition systems, especially some of those developed in the Far East, have demonstrated this very clearly.

It is surely true that children learn best in the presence of a teacher who is constantly on hand to encourage, cajole, instruct, inform and guide. In the primary classroom children simply are not just given instruction and then sent away to practise on their own.

Requests for Extra Work

None of the above should imply that a child who asks for homework be turned away. Some teachers do refuse, often simply pointing out that 'We don't give homework at this school'. There is probably nothing wrong with doing this, and it could be a simple and effective way of avoiding any kind of homework-related problem. Another teacher, however, might find it difficult to turn down a child who is obviously enthusiastic to carry on something started in class.

Compulsory Homework

If, in a particular school, a teacher has to operate a compulsory homework policy, what is he or she to do about children who fail to do their homework or who do it in an unsatisfactory way? The problem here is that a teacher who is building a good relationship with the class may be forced into admonishing or actually punishing children with whom he or she has no other quarrel at all. It is quite difficult, in fact, to see how a compulsory homework policy can be enforced at primary level at all. It is difficult enough at secondary level, where the habit of homework is more firmly established, and where there is usually a structure of sanctions for children who disobey school rules.

Learning Difficulties

Formal homework can rarely, if ever, be an effective means of helping a child through learning difficulties. By and large, problems have to be overcome in class. Although planned home–school co-operation, of course *is* successful.

Parental Requests

Homework is often requested by parents. In each case, some thought ought to be given as to the reason for the request. Do the parents, for example, hope that a dose of homework will enable a slow-learning child to catch up? Are they asking for social reasons, because the school down the road gives homework?

Integrating Work

The real problem about homework is that, as a concept, it sits uneasily on the primary-school ethos. For a child engrossed in a cross-curricular project, or in putting together a folder about the books he or she has read, the distinction between 'school work' and 'homework' does not really exist. The work commutes with the child between classroom and home – and ideally both parents and teachers will contribute to it in some way. Thus the notion of 'setting homework' becomes entirely redundant.

To be fair, the same pattern is developing in secondary schools. 'Coursework' – for GCSE, or for projects lower down the school – makes the same kind of informal home–school links as does the primary-school project, and in its own way starts to make the old 'homework diary' redundant.

13
WHO'S WHO

The roles filled by many of the people who are part of school life are only vaguely understood even by quite experienced teachers. This is a brief explanation of some of them.

Inspectors

There are, essentially, two kinds of inspectors. Local-authority inspectors are, as the title suggests, employed by the local authority to oversee the running of the authority's schools. They have a variety of tasks to do largely with ensuring that schools deliver a proper curriculum. Authorities organize their inspectors in various ways. There may be 'phase' inspectors – (primary, secondary, further) or there may be 'subject' inspectors (maths, English, etc.). Sometimes there will be both, and occasionally the organization is looser and less clearly defined. A school may also have a 'pastoral' inspector who combines with other functions that or looking after a group of schools. A probationer teacher will usually be assigned to the care of an inspector, who may visit regularly or who may delegate the duty to a peripatetic teacher or tutor.

As well as local-authority inspectors there are 'HMIs' (Her Majesty's Inspectors of Schools). These are independent of the local authority, reporting directly to the Secretary of State. A classroom teacher may go for years without having an HMI in his or her room. When one does come it might be as part of a brief visit to the school in pursuit of some particular aim – a general look at primary history, for example – or because the school is being subjected to a full inspection by a team of HMI.

HMI are amazingly thorough. If there is a full inspection a group of HMI will stay in school for a week, and for just about the whole of that time they will be observing classroom work. They follow up with a report – verbally to the head and to the governors, and eventually in writing in published form.

Advisers

Employed by local authorities, advisers are often simply inspectors with a different name. The difference of title usually indicates a desire to emphasize the supportive nature of the job. Some authorities have both advisers and inspectors, in which case the titles adequately describe the differing roles.

Advisory Teachers

These should not be confused with advisers or with inspectors. Their status is not so high, and they are emphatically co-equal with other teachers. Usually, indeed, they are classroom teachers who have chosen to spend some time in an advisory role. Commonly, they will return to the classroom after a few years. Support for probationary teachers is often given by advisory teachers rather than directly by advisers or inspectors.

Peripatetic Teachers

These are teachers who go from school to school teaching a specialist subject. The most commonly met 'peri' is the one who teachers a musical instrument. Because they work on a timetable that takes in lots of schools, they often take children from class at inconvenient times. It is important, however, to understand the constraints within which they work – and, of course, the tremendous contribution they make. All too often they work in isolation from the rest of the school curriculum. If this is so, then they may respond well to an approach from a class teacher to try to make links between what the child does with the peri and what he or she does in class.

Educational Psychologist

The 'Ed psych' is a highly qualified professional. To be an ed psych you have to be an experienced qualified teacher, have a first degree in psychology and a higher degree in educational psychology. Ed psychs often have particular specialities – 'gifted' children, perhaps, or particular kinds of special need. Much of their work these days is taken up with the requirements of the special-needs procedure. This is a pity, because they have much to offer by way of general advice to teachers. An invitation to an ed psych simply to observe a class, for example, can provide some interesting and helpful follow-up discussion.

Education Welfare Officer or Education Social Worker

There used to be 'attendance officers' who were simply police for school attendance. This image still lives on in some ways, and most EWOs spend a lot of time on attendance problems. They will, however, support other forms of home–school liaison, and have a role to play when there is, for example, worry about possible child abuse.

Governors

School governors have wide-ranging responsibilities, and meet regularly with the head and, often, other senior teachers. All too often, however, they meet other teachers only infrequently. One way round this is to ask the teacher-governor to try to organize some kind of 'get-to-know-you' session. The teacher-governor, incidentally, is a vital link between the staffroom and the decision-makers. He or she should be seeking out issues for governors' meetings and reporting back afterwards.

Education Officers

At the summit of the local authority's bureaucratic structure is a chief education officer. At the next couple of levels down will be a group of deputy and assistant officers with various responsibilities. The one most commonly encountered by classroom teachers is the staffing officer. This is the person to speak to when there are real worries about conditions of service that cannot be resolved in school. Usually the staffing officer is supported by a clerical staff, and the senior clerk (whatever his or her exact title) is a key ally for any teacher with a problem. Teachers should try hard to be friendly and supportive to staffing-office staff!

Caretakers

The school caretaker carries a responsibility entirely disproportionate to the level of salary attached to the job. A good caretaker enhances the life of a school. A lazy or disgruntled caretaker causes problems for everyone. A classroom teacher should try to make a friend of the caretaker – and of the cleaner who looks after his or her room – but should also be firm about maintenance of cleaning standards and any potential interference with his or her work and responsibilities as a teacher. All problems should be referred up – and pursued relentlessly if nothing is done!

Consideration for the caretaker and cleaners involves

- consulting them about access to the school at weekends or in holidays;
- apologizing when there has been a particularly messy classroom activity;
- coming to a working arrangement with the cleaner when children or teacher are going to work late in the classroom; and
- putting them in the picture about special events, especially if there are going to be consequences for their work.

Secretary

The school secretary is an important ally. They are usually over-worked, however, as well as seeing their first responsibility as being to the head. The worst thing a junior teacher can do is to treat the secretary casually – asking, perhaps, to do eight pages of typing 'as soon as possible'.

Visiting Work-people

Sooner or later, a teacher will experience the arrival of a group of workers in overalls who proceed, without warning, to do very noisy things just outside the door or on the roof. Any remonstrations with them should be limited. Serious complaints should go to the head. After that, some sort of working compromise should be sorted out. They are earning a living, after all.

Part V: Appendix

FURTHER READING

Ainscow, M. and Muncey, J. (1989) *Meeting Individual Needs*, David Fulton (about special needs and 'problem' kids).

Bastiani, J. (1989) *Working with Parents, a Whole-School Approach*, NFER-Nelson, Windsor (beyond the PTA – how to run the curriculum with parent support).

Besag, E. (1989) *Bullies and Victims in Schools*. Open University Press, Milton Keynes (sensitive, realistic and highly practical in offering strategies for coping).

Kutnick, P.J. (1989) *Relationships in the Primary School Classroom*. Paul Chapman, London (socio-psychological research into how the network of classroom relationships affects learning).

Shuard, H. and Rothery, A. (eds.) (1984) *Children Reading Mathematics*. John Murray, London (the task of reading the text can be a barrier to maths progress).

INDEX